ELECTRONIC
RESUME
REVOLUTION

ELECTRONIC RESUME REVOLUTION

CREATE A WINNING RESUME FOR THE NEW WORLD OF JOB SEEKING

Joyce Lain Kennedy and Thomas J. Morrow

JOHN WILEY & SONS, INC.

New York • Chichester • Brisbane • Toronto • Singapore

This text is printed on acid-free paper.

Copyright © 1994 by Joyce Lain Kennedy and Thomas J. Morrow.

Published by John Wiley & Sons, Inc.

All rights reserved. Published simultaneously in Canada.

Reproduction or translation of any part of this work beyond
that permitted by Section 107 or 108 of the 1976 United
States Copyright Act without the permission of the copyright
owner is unlawful. Requests for permission or further
information should be addressed to the Permissions Department,
John Wiley & Sons, Inc., 605 Third Avenue, New York, NY
10158-0012.

This publication is designed to provide accurate and
authoritative information in regard to the subject
matter covered. It is sold with the understanding that
the publisher is not engaged in rendering legal, accounting,
or other professional services. If legal advice or other
expert assistance is required, the services of a competent
professional person should be sought. *From a Declaration
of Principles jointly adopted by a Committee of the
American Bar Association and a Committee of Publishers.*

Library of Congress Cataloging in Publication Data:

Kennedy, Joyce Lain.
     Electronic resume revolution : create a winning resume
  for the new world of job seeking / by Joyce Lain Kennedy and
  Thomas J. Morrow.
        p.   cm.
     Includes bibliographical references.
     ISBN 0-471-59822-4 (cloth : acid-free paper). — ISBN
  0-471-59823-2 (pbk. : acid-free paper)
     1. Resumés (Employment)—Technological innovations.   2. Resumés
  (Employment)—Data processing.   I. Morrow, Thomas J.   II. Title.
  HF5383.K42   1994
  650.14'0285—dc20   93-5191

Printed in the United States of America

10 9 8 7 6 5 4 3 2 1

For

William A. Kennedy

> My beloved husband, who helped
> me sail on an argosy of magic.
>
> J.L.K.

For I dipped into the future, far as human eye could see,
Saw the vision of the world, and all the wonder that would be;
Saw the heavens fill with commerce, argosies of magic sails,
Pilots of the purple twilight, dropping down with costly bales.

—Alfred, Lord Tennyson

Rosalee A. Morrow

> My wonderfully patient and loving wife,
> who laughs at my jokes and who helped
> me to see a whole new life.
>
> T.J.M.

Foreword

It's an old story: Job seekers say they constantly are frustrated by an employment process so antiquated and subjective that, despite their obvious qualifications, they are denied fair attention from companies. Employers complain that applicants continually fight the system, thus making it difficult to identify and hire the right people.

One factor frequently mentioned as a major obstacle in the hiring process is the resume. Without a doubt, it is the most important document in your job search—it is a key ingredient in more than 90 percent of all new hires. Potential employers, friends, employment agents, and other people whom you contact will make the inevitable request, "Send me a copy of your resume." Questions concerning resume usage, validity, and style are simply endless.

Even human resource experts have trouble agreeing on the resume's value and format. Should the document be one, two, three pages—or more? What type of information should it contain: duties, responsibilities, accomplishments? Must goals and objectives be included? Is a qualifications summary helpful? Where should education be placed? Are employment dates and affiliations with every employer required?

This may surprise you: There are as many answers as there are questions. Weary participants in the employment process often lament, "There must be a better way," but there is no escaping the fact that the resume document is the universally accepted method for you to describe your background and obtain a job interview.

Unfortunately, everyone who ever has looked for a job sees himself or herself as some sort of authority on the topic. That's why the occasional job seeker is overwhelmed with well-meaning advice, much of it suspect. As a result, resume creation often is not handled well. Most experts agree that poor resumes, along with a lack of interviewing skills and a failure to network, are at the root of ineffective job searches.

But now, the dynamics of the employment process are changing.

As the philosophy of "lean and mean" has exerted itself on human resource departments, HR specialists have had to do more with less. This operating mandate especially applies in employment organizations, which, in this time of a high unemployment rate, have been overwhelmed with applicants.

For progressive recruiters, the solution has been found in the use of computers, optical scanners, and other electronic equipment, in combination with creative software programs. Technology in the 1990s is making a major impact on the hiring function.

Hiring Processes in Transition

Corporate employment departments, executive search firms, and employment agencies are changing their methods of personnel selection as they install or update user-friendly personnel retrieval systems. These changes are enabling them to identify candidates for their openings without spending hundreds of hours wading through stacks of resumes. The initial screening no longer has to be a dull task performed by bleary-eyed recruiters and research analysts whose biases affect their objectivity. Technology, with reliable accuracy, has replaced humans in the initial screening process.

In the past year, we have witnessed numerous converts to this new method of recruitment and, as the word spreads and more sophisticated equipment is developed for performing recruiting work, it will become an accepted process for most employers. "What did we ever do before the fax?" has become a very common question in today's business environment. For employment department staff, the electronic resume soon will be receiving similar acclaim.

I am not suggesting you should throw away your current chronological or functional resume. This document will continue to play an important part in your search, especially in employment and information interviews. Instead, I am recommending the use of two versions: an electronic resume to help you attract the attention of the robotic recruiter, and a traditional paper copy to assist in selling yourself in face-to-face real-people situations.

In today's economy, everyone is concerned about his or her future in the workplace. Mergers, acquisitions, divestitures, layoffs, and other corporate changes have disrupted many careers at all levels. The rules of the past in regard to employment no longer apply.

Technology: Your Career Insurance

Job security requires being good at what you do and making certain that others are aware of it—both inside and outside the organization. By entering your electronic resume into the sourcing systems of professional recruiters, you are buying a little insurance to cover the responsibility you must assume for your own career wellness. This alert approach should result in attaining the visibility you have always desired.

Some people may insist that a specially prepared cover letter will be sufficient to solve the electronic dilemma. Nothing could be further from the truth. This correspondence is intended to complement your work biography, not to contradict it. Any significant change from the resume content will be viewed as last-minute patchwork that has little validity. Even though it may be tailored specifically to a situation, it will have the negative impact of a preprinted letter. You never want to convey to any employer an initial impression that you prefer shortcuts over hard work.

By following the suggestions offered in this groundbreaking book, you will be well on the way to gaining the competitive edge that will put you ahead of other job seekers. The authors have compiled an enviable record in the employment and career planning fields. Their advice is well founded and hits directly in the center of the job search bull's-eye.

This book is quite different than anything you have read or been told previously. Read it. Absorb it. Apply it. If you pay close attention to the instructions given here, you will go to the head of the class. Be prepared. The future of The Resume Revolution is NOW.

JOHN D. ERDLEN, EXECUTIVE DIRECTOR

Wellesley, Massachusetts

John D. Erdlen is executive director of the Northeast Human Resources Association, and a former executive director of the Employment Management Association. Mr. Erdlen is also president of The Erdlen Bograd Group, an outplacement and human resource consulting firm in Wellesley, Massachusetts.

Trademarks

For readability, in this work vendor names are not set in capital letters, nor are the signs indicating trademarks or service marks used. All known marks are listed here. This list is not necessarily complete. Any use of marked names, whether on this list or not, is editorial and to the benefit of the mark holder. The marks appear as they are used by the companies holding the marks.

Mark	Mark Holder
Abra Cadabra™	Abra Cadabra Software, Inc.
Caere®	Caere Corporation
Calera®	Calera Recognition Systems
cors™	cors, Inc.
Job Bank USA™	Job Bank USA, Inc.
kiNEXUS™	Information Kinetics, Inc.
RESTRAC™	MicroTrac Systems, Inc.
Resumix™	Resumix, Inc.
SkillSearch®	SkillSearch Corporation
SmartSearch2™	Advanced Personnel Systems
SS2™	Advanced Personnel Systems
Unix®	AT&T Bell Laboratories
WordPerfect®	WordPerfect Corporation

Acknowledgments

By different methods different people excel. Our method is to work with excellent colleagues. We express sincere appreciation to these *keypeople*.

EDITORIAL SUPPORT TEAM

Muriel Wallace Turner, Sun Features Inc.
Gayle Leslie Bryant, The Kennedy Office
Laura Ruekberg, Editorial Consultant

ADVISERS

James M. Lemke, Resumix
Jane Paradiso, Bell Atlantic
Charles Borwick, Restrac
Douglas F. Coull, SmartSearch2
Patrick O'Leary, United Parcel Service Airlines
Lars D. Perkins, Restrac
Jean Andrews, The Consulting Team
Daniel J. Harriger, Abra Cadabra
Peter D. Weddle, Job Bank USA
Mark Gisleson, Gisleson Writing Services
Richard D. Miller, SmartSearch2
Lerry "Nick" Nicholson, Systems Professional
Cynthia D. Diers, Association of Human Resource Systems Professionals
Stephen V. Rice, Information Science Research Institute, University of Nevada, Las Vegas

RECRUITER

Eva M. June, Walling, June & Associates

PUBLISHER

At John Wiley & Sons: **Mike Hamilton, Fred Nachbaur, Elena Paperny, Karl Weber, Mary Daniello, Linda Indig, Peter Clifton.**
At Publications Development Company: **Maryan Malone, Nancy Marcus Land, Denise Netardus.**

Contents

Contents

ELECTRONIC
RESUME
REVOLUTION

Introduction

Computers read resumes differently than people do. They are making it easier than ever in history for employers to comparison shop among job seekers.

If there's a hair's difference between job seekers, computers can split it. Computers compare every measurable differential—every shade of meaning in experience, skills, education, previous employers, and career achievement.

When we began researching this book more than a year ago, we knew that large changes were taking place in America's corporate hiring halls. What we didn't know was that, in scale, the changes are as significant as when the Industrial Age was replaced by the Information Age a few decades ago.

Computers are doing for employers what giant shopping malls have done for consumers. Instead of running all over town to one merchant here and another there, trying to remember what one is offering and the other isn't, shoppers can now move back and forth very quickly among stores and their competing neighbors. The shopping mall competition has sharpened consumers' bargaining awareness and buying power.

Similarly, employers operating computers armed with the right software can compare notes on thousands of applicants faster than you can say, "Live one online."

Millions of workers today are being entered into hundreds of *automated applicant tracking systems*, which are similar to the theater industry's casting directories. They are being used by employers and executive search firms, and by independent resume databases operated by commercial enterprises, colleges, and the federal government.

The technology is rewriting the rules on how to find jobs during the 1990s.

Not only is the technology making it more effortless than ever for employers to compare people, but the timing is perfect for the use of new systems. As the United States gears down from the boom years following World War II, employers are looking around and finding themselves in the driver's seat.

People who hire can now afford to be very demanding in their requests for specific kinds of sharply honed skills and well-defined levels of education. Precise resume search and retrieval addresses this need. Employers know precisely what qualifications they want and they're asking for them. The automated systems are well equipped to meet a heightened demand for very specific kinds of applicants, and they offer the capacity to compare them at a glance.

It was not always thus. In the past, employers had to manually sort through stacks and stacks of paper resumes. Even the most qualified applicants didn't always get invited in for personal inspection because some of their qualifications were overlooked. Good resumes may have gone untouched simply because they were too far down in the pile.

Computers take their work very seriously. Compared to humans, computers are more thorough, more specific, and more objective—three good reasons why a new approach has to be taken in planning, writing, and submitting your resume.

That's what this book is all about—how to *use* computers and the breathtaking technology that is upon us. Our guide is for people who do not intend to get left behind in the wake of the new technology that is changing how resumes wend their way through corporate America today.

As we frankly admit in our companion book, *Electronic Job Search Revolution*, which gives you the big picture of how the nation's employment processes are changing, we are not gifted in technical areas. Ultimately, this may be for the best because we don't know enough about the workings of technology to get too carried away with it. Our interest is in how the technology affects the chances of your resume winning you a job interview, and how to improve your odds.

We tell you what you need to understand about producing a new kind of resume that can lick any computer and survive to be read by human eyes. We explain how scanners and optical character recognition (OCR) systems work, and what effect they might have on your resume. We give you loads of tips and keyword skills you can use to make sure you're branded with the right labels—the labels computers look for when they are matching applicants with jobs.

As you read, you'll notice that *Electronic Resume Revolution* answers questions abundantly:

▶ Why must I know about automated technology when I am applying to small businesses that probably don't have it yet? See Chapter 1.

▶ Why will scanners and OCR software cause me to change anything about my resume? See Chapter 2.

▶ Keywords are at the center of the new resume rules, but what are the right keywords? See Chapter 3.

▶ Why can't I use underlining or rules in my resume anymore? Do I submit three pages, two, or one? Must I go back beyond 10 years in my experience section? See Chapter 4.

▶ What is a keyword resume format? Why would I want one? See Chapter 5.

▶ When computers can read my resume and figure out what job I fit, is it still useful to personalize my resume for a job I really want? See Chapter 6.

▶ Under the new rules, how can I learn what a lot of keyword resumes look like? See Chapter 7.

▶ What if I have to perform my resume in front of a television camera? See Chapter 8.

▶ What can I do if no computer seems to want me? See Chapter 9.

Remember, computers read resumes differently than people do. They are making it easier than ever before in history for employers to comparison shop among job seekers. This book opens your understanding toward becoming the best that money can buy.

1

The Resume That's Sweeping the Nation

Now! You Need a New Style Resume Because Computers Read Differently Than People Do

New technology is changing forever the way to apply for a job in America.

The reasons aren't hard to discover. Job seekers are flooding employers with paper resumes and, after a decade of downsizing, companies have fewer human resource specialists to manage the hiring process.

This chapter overviews the explosive speed at which hiring automation is moving, notes advantages and disadvantages to job seekers, and suggests a simple method for becoming skilled in keyword searching.

It explains why you now may want to have not one but two core resumes: one meant for human eyes only, the other for the eyes of a computer.

Sally Jessy Raphael speaks movingly of joblessness in her very human and inspiring autobiography, *Sally*. She says flexibility was her viewpoint after leaving Miami for New York to land a broadcasting job in the nation's top media market.

"Every week I'd keep trying to sell my way into a radio or TV job. 'I'll be a disc jockey,' I said, pulling out my disc jockey resume.

When that didn't work, I'd change the resume. I had a disc jockey resume, a news resume and a television resume at the ready, in case someone needed me."

Sally doesn't say whether she performed her occupational hat trick for the *same* radio or TV station. Her legions of fans are just grateful that whatever it was that she did *worked*. Job application agility, under the old rules, was a mark of resourcefulness and a harbinger of ultimate success.

Until now, submitting multiple resumes to the same employer was perfectly fine, even recommended. Each version was tilted to accent a different set of skills, and the broadband technique was supposed to cover all the bases. Like buying more than one sweepstakes ticket, multiple resumes were thought to increase your chances of being hired because, by varying your presentation, you were helping the decision maker visualize how you could fit into more than one particular role.

Because each resume was stashed in a different file—"software engineer" in one and "information specialist" in another—chances were slim that anyone would tie you to all your occupational aliases.

Jody Pitman, systems marketing manager . . . also known as Jody Pitman, human resource manager . . . a.k.a. Jody Pitman, promotion director . . . a.k.a. Jody Pitman, management consultant.

Who could keep track of you in all those files, assuming your resumes made it past the wastepaper basket? You probably were safe presenting yourself as a public accountant on one resume and as an internal auditing specialist on another. Not anymore.

Today, there's a real danger in sending multiple resumes to the same company when each presents you as a different and perhaps seemingly fictional character. A reviewer is watching and that reviewer has chips for brains. Technology now makes it possible for a computer to compare documents as quickly as word about the latest firing gets around your office.

"When you double-up or triple-up on resumes, you will probably be spotted as a person who is unfocused or, worse, not straightforward," says James M. Lemke, director of national accounts for Resumix, Inc., a leading maker of automated applicant tracking systems in Santa Clara, California.

"Recruiters can instantly pull to the screen every mention of your name," explains Lemke, who, before joining Resumix, worked for 20 years in human resource management at several major corporations, including Walt Disney Imagineering in Glendale, California.

"If, when your multiple resumes are compiled in one central file, you don't look as though you are the same person on all of them, you'll raise questions. Either you're the original Renaissance person—a real Michelangelo of industry—or you're unrealistic about what you can do, or your nose is growing," Lemke says.

When that doubt arises, other human resource specialists agree with Lemke that you're likely to be passed by without much thought.

"You're seen as a risk, and in today's market, anyone doing screening really doesn't want to hire a risk. In most cases, there are just too many people who want the good jobs," says Jean Andrews, director of operations for The Consulting Team, Inc., a nationwide human resource systems consulting firm headquartered in West Palm Beach, Florida.

"A variation of the multiple resume tactic," Andrews explains, "is the applicant who sends the identical resume to everyone in the place: the president, the vice president, the human resource director, the stockholder relations director, the hiring manager—anyone whose name the job seeker can find who has the remotest chance of influencing a hiring decision.

"That strategy, which sometimes used to work because managers didn't always get together on resumes," Andrews adds, "now may get you tagged as someone who is desperate, who is flailing about wildly. This can work against you because you'll not be seen as one who is a hot candidate, but a kind of loose cannon hoping for a hit."

OLD RULES CAN HURT YOU

Ten years ago, applicant tracking technology barely existed. Although it has been around since the early 1970s, it wasn't until the late 1980s that it became sophisticated and widely adopted.

The new cautions on sending multiple resumes are only the tip of the iceberg in technology's rewrite of the hiring process—a rewrite that is racing across the nation as you read these pages.

Another old rule of presenting yourself that may now hurt your chances is heavy reliance on action verbs in your resume. How often have you been advised to put your resume "in active form"—to use active verbs, not passive prose?

Under the old rules, when you were certain your resume would be read only by human eyes, it was correct, as one smart career counselor put it, "to release the energy hidden in your written accomplishments" with words like these:

> accelerated, arbitrated, centralized, consulted, converted, coordinated, created, designed, developed, diagnosed, directed, evaluated, expanded, improved, increased, launched, led, managed, minimized,

negotiated, organized, presented, programmed, reduced, replaced, researched, resolved, restructured, simplified, slashed, sold, solved, streamlined, strengthened, supervised, taught, took charge, took over, trained, upgraded, wrote.

Further good advice—under the old rules—was to avoid jargon, and to put your abilities into short, generic phrases that everyone could understand, like these:

Analyzing and solving problems.
Writing computer programs.

When a Friend Finds You a Job

Peg Donovan returned to her native Oregon after a number of years spent working in the corporate world in California. She found re-establishing contacts in the Portland, Oregon, area somewhat difficult.

"When I first moved back to Portland, it was hard to break in and get my network going again after being gone for a few years," recalls Donovan. "I was sending out three to five resumes every day, hoping I'd hit something. I got one or two responses out of 40 or so."

Eventually, Donovan landed on her feet at a high-tech company in the Portland area. The job turned out to be a less-than-ideal match, and Donovan decided in late April that it was time to move on. She shared that desire—and an updated resume—with a friend who is in the temporary help business.

In May, Donovan received a letter acknowledging her application from Nike, the popular sports equipment manufacturer headquartered in nearby Beaverton. What application? Donovan hadn't yet applied to Nike—although it was the number-one place she wanted to work.

"When I got an acknowledgment letter from Nike—I was surprised," recalls Donovan. "I didn't know they had my resume, but I knew my friend has contacts there [Nike] because of her work, so I knew it had to be her doing."

Nike's applicant tracking system was newly up and running when the company received Donovan's resume, and hers was one of the first to navigate the system and one of the first to pop up.

Donovan now works for Nike as an administrative assistant to the corporate controller.

"Being a prudent person, I had been interviewing with another company when I received the Nike acknowledgment letter," she says. "I was overjoyed. Nike is what I really wanted! Everybody wants to work here. They have a great reputation in this community. They care about their people—they're solid."

Planning and organizing.
Designing and teaching training classes.

All of this, in its day, was wonderful advice. It still is—when writing a paper resume and organizing your thoughts in anticipation of a job interview.

But it's usually terrible advice for constructing the new style, computer-friendly, *scannable* resume being embraced by cost-conscious corporate America. Industry jargon is the coin of the realm. It's just one more example of why you must learn to think differently about your resume.

Employment America has a new best-friend combination: resume scanning software and automated applicant tracking systems. For short, the technology is merely called *applicant tracking systems.* By any name, it will have an impact on your life.

ELECTRONIC TRAFFIC COPS:
APPLICANT TRACKING SYSTEMS

They don't tell you to your face, but the new automated applicant tracking systems do tell you where to go. That is, they tell your resume where to go.

You belong here, in the product manager file. And you there, get on line in the administrative assistant category. Whatever you do, don't either of you move until I signal you to come back out.

The tracking systems are bossy little pieces of technology in the sense that they are electronic traffic cops telling your resume where to go and when to come back. If you find that thought annoying, consider the alternative: On the paper farms that employment offices have become, without automation your resume is likely to be plowed under and buried. Until the early 1990s, job hunters who were assured their resume would be kept on file knew an empty promise when they heard one.

"It was only last year [1992] that we escaped a half-century dependency on the old metal file drawer," says Chris Dorr, manager of human resources at MCI Telecommunications, Inc., in Richardson, Texas.

Quoted in *Personnel Journal,* a trade publication for the human resource industry, Dorr says that, besides dealing with the back-wrenching work of filing thousands of resumes, if the clerk assigning them to the appropriate category got the coding wrong, or if there was a backlog of resumes waiting to be coded, "a lot of new resumes were as good as lost."

Now, computers do the legwork and, like hunting for tools in a tidy garage, it's easier to find things once they're put away. MCI installed SmartSearch2, a resume scanning and applicant tracking system marketed by Advanced Personnel Systems in Oceanside, California. No longer do MCI recruiters have to interpret resumes to figure out which job categories they fit, or wear out a photocopier to make sets of resumes for everyone who wants them.

The technology—an astounding experience the first time you watch it work—benefits employers in other ways, beyond keeping on top of all the paper resumes. With resume scanning and automated tracking, "It's easy to consider *all* candidates for a position, not just those whose resumes were on the recruiter's desk at any one time," explains Lars D. Perkins, president of MicroTrac Systems, Inc., the Dedham, Massachusetts, company that developed the Restrac employment automation system.

Employment applications (relatives of resumes) also reflect potent new technology. Perkins, a pioneer of the industry and one of the first to put the technology on a PC, has introduced an applicant tracking system with kiosks (dedicated personal computers) that allows walk-in applicants to enter their applications directly into the system without human intervention.

Restrac, Resumix, and SmartSearch2 are three of the 20 or so U.S. companies we found that sell resume scanning software and automated applicant tracking systems. Restrac has announced a strategic business alliance with PeopleSoft, Inc., of Walnut Creek, California, a leader in business application software.

Resumix has announced a partnership agreement to integrate its products into the business application software marketed by SAP America, Inc., a subsidiary of SAP AG, one of the world's largest software developers.

Each applicant tracking system has unique features. Some are far more technologically advanced than others. At least two systems incorporate artificial intelligence, or expert systems, but most do not. We get to that issue in the next chapter.

To gain an elementary level of understanding, Figure 1–1 will show you the main idea on which all these systems are based.

Resumes arrive in the office and are fed through a scanner. The scanner sends a picture of the document to a computer equipped with optical character recognition (OCR) software. The software translates the resume data into a universal computer language called ASCII.

The computer "reads" each resume quickly, identifies keywords, and, based on the keywords it reads, stashes the resume in an appropriate database file. Apples are zipped to the apple file, oranges to the orange file, and so forth.

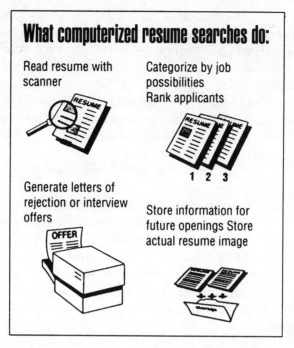

Figure 1–1   How Computerized Resume Searches Work (Reprinted by permission of Small Business News.)

When a job opening occurs, an employer tells the applicant tracking system the keywords associated with the position and instructs it to fetch the resumes that incorporate matching keywords.

*Go down to the apple file and bring back all the **Granny Smiths** and **Romes**. Enter the orange file and bring back the **Navels** but leave the Valencias.*

Keywords—**Granny Smiths, Romes, Navels,** in this whimsical example—are the essential characteristics required to do the job: education, experience, skills, knowledge, abilities. Keywords are the "wants" in help-wanted ads.

It is not an overstatement to say keywords can change your life. Instead of asking for your driver's license, the electronic traffic cops say, "Show me your *keywords.*"

IN THE NAME OF COMPETITIVENESS

Are you wondering why all this unsettling technology is happening during *your* career? Why is hiring being reduced to an infinite stream of zeros and ones that computers crunch to accomplish their digital duties? Whatever happened to the human factors that industrial chieftains have trumpeted for years—ideas, toughness, tenaciousness, and other invisible strengths? What is the world coming to?

The world is coming to cutthroat competitiveness. You've probably noticed that our recent economic trouble isn't a typical slowdown. It's a worldwide change of new technology and global competition. It involves all industrial nations, even the new ones.

For U.S. businesses, the new competitiveness that's changing the culture in which we work is bottom-line-driven. Be lean and mean. Squeeze, trim, cut, chop, prune, sever—do it and survive!

The new stripped-down strategies have dealt hordes of American workers a knockout blow.

The blood bath is far from over. Innovation is combining with competition to alter the very structure of many industries.

When telephone companies improve video teleconferencing, airlines and hotels see part of their basic businesses gone for good.

When U.S. automotive businesses move operations to Mexico, not only workers but their bosses wave farewell to jobs that now belong to the Third World.

Against this background, abetted by the takeover robber barons of the 1980s who wrecked companies for personal gain, U.S. corporations ditched well over 1 million middle managers and professionals in the late 1980s and early 1990s.

That's only a corner of the picture: the total body count between 1987 and 1992 is 5.6 million laid-off workers.

We don't have the figures on how many of those departed workers were human resource specialists, but anecdotal evidence suggests human resource departments suffered heavy casualties.

At the same time, companies are swamped with resumes from people who want to work for them. It is not unusual for popular employers to receive 5,000 and more unsolicited resumes monthly. Not enough people are left standing in human resource departments to face that level of onslaught, if they use the old methods.

A California defense contractor recently slashed its human resource department from fourteen to two specialists and then ran a one-inch ad in the *Los Angeles Times* for an accountant. The ad drew 600 replies! You guessed it—the company now has an automated applicant tracking system.

Competitiveness and innovation have forged two 1990s trends that seem joined at the hip: fewer employees are available to evaluate growing numbers of applicants.

HIRING AUTOMATION IS EXPLODING

The convergence of the "fewer human resources employees" and "more applicants" trends has created a void that employment systems technology is rushing to fill.

Automation that can save hundreds of thousands or even millions of dollars over a period of years, resume scanning software, and automated applicant tracking systems are taking the country's business world by storm.

KPMG Peat Marwick, one of the Big Six accounting firms recently released a national study titled "Human Resource Information Technology in the 1990s."

In this study, large companies are described as having more than 5,000 employees; medium-size companies have between 500 and 5,000 employees; and small companies are those with fewer than 500 employees. The Peat Marwick survey of technology in use is not directly comparable to studies of employers that use scannable technology, but it is in the same ballpark.

The survey measured two automated functions of interest: (1) applicant tracking and (2) employee skills inventory:

| | Percentage of Companies Using | |
Company Size	Applicant Tracking	Employee Skills Inventory
Large (5,000+)	55%	36%
Medium (500–5,000)	44	26
Small (1–499)	14	6

The data were gathered in 1990; the numbers are probably much higher now.

Hard studies of precise usage haven't yet surfaced, but they are certain to be forthcoming within the next few years. The word in human resource circles is of wildfire growth in applicant tracking systems.

How blazingly fast is the growth? Resumix's James Lemke, although not a disinterested observer, anticipates that a whopping 80 percent of medium-size to large employers will process resumes by computer before the century is finished.

We think Lemke's right on target. Along with its focus on the bottom line, business has developed a warm, fuzzy feeling for computers in general.

Four out of five executives (81 percent) firmly believe that computers have increased the productivity of their staffs. Nearly nine out of 10 (89 percent) agree that computers have increased the speed of information flow within their companies, and eight out of 10 (81 percent) report increased accuracy.

These findings come from a recent nationwide survey by The Olsten Corporation of 1,481 management information systems executives representing a range of industries. They provided their views on computer productivity, staffing, and training issues.

Personal computers are used at 94 percent of the companies surveyed; in addition, 78 percent of the companies still use more centralized systems, such as those requiring mainframes. Three out of four also have some type of local area network. Of the companies surveyed, 94 percent use computers for database management.

Even in a sluggish economy, 7 out of 10 (69 percent) companies increased their budgets for information systems and office automation.

SMALL COMPANIES TURNING TO SERVICE BUREAUS

A recent study by Cognetics, Inc., a Cambridge, Massachusetts, economics research firm, plugs numbers into what we've been hearing for several years: By headcount, the hiring action in the United States is in the small business sector.

Between 1987 and 1992, companies with fewer than 100 employees added a net 5,864,000 jobs, while large companies lost a net 2,320,000 jobs. The small companies pay "average or better wages"; the jobs cut by the large companies were "high-paying."

In essence, the power and money tracks are more frequently found at large companies, but small companies offer pleasant tracks that pay well and there are too many of them to ignore.

A logical question: Isn't hiring automation at small companies light years away? Not necessarily. It's true that because large companies have greater investments in technology, their human resource departments tend to be more computerized than those of smaller enterprises. Many small businesses that need to bring people aboard can't justify the expense of staffing automation. Even so, there may be nowhere to hide from technology or to duck the machines that will read your resume.

In the 1990s, small businesses—and cash-tight larger companies—are farming out the task of finding people to hire. They buy the services offered by independent resume database services, such as the Career Placement Registry, cors, Job Bank USA, kiNexus, and SkillSearch.

They also turn to service bureaus such as Advanced Personnel Systems (APS), which offers the entire human resource function.

Douglas F. Coull, APS's president, explains that the service bureau portion of his company is called SS2 Online. For the cost of buying a system, companies can contract for two or four years of advanced scanning-based resume management and applicant tracking services. Client companies can use their existing PCs and SS2 Online handles all the technical headaches.

Many client companies, Coull says, lease first and then buy the systems outright once they find out they can't live without them. Client information—including your resume—is safeguarded through an elaborate safety system.

Just because you are applying to a small company, don't assume your resume will not be read by a computer.

NAKED ON THE SCREEN

Revolutions have a way of starting in the Northeast, and the applicant tracking system revolution is no exception.

Quoted in the *Wall Street Journal*, MicroTrac's president, Lars Perkins, jokes that the resume destined to cross the most desks is one mentioning many job titles and capabilities, even if it says, "I have never been president, I don't program in Basic, C, or Pascal." Words nobody searches for, Perkins says, include "verbs like 'managed' and 'empowered.'"

Perkins' observations, although humorous, have validity for many automated applicant tracking systems. However, advanced systems won't fall for such tomfoolery, and neither will human recruiters after they take a closer look at such a resume.

Perkins' point zeros in on the heart of the new style scannable resume: keyword searching. Remember the string of action verbs—from *accelerated* to *wrote*—mentioned earlier in this chapter?

Restrac user Edward Gagen, manager of recruiting at Ortho Pharmaceutical, a division of Johnson & Johnson, in Raritan, New Jersey, expands on the changing rules. "Resumes must be written carefully to ensure that they pop up at the right time. Resume writers used to sell action verbs. With scannable resumes, it's nouns."

Marc S. Miller, a management consultant in New Rochelle, New York, and a recognized authority in human resource information systems, agrees that a focus on keywords and nouns is the secret to writing forceful, computer-friendly resumes.

"It very much matters how resumes are written for scanner reading. Suppose a company is recruiting a chemical engineer. Keywords identify the processes the engineer must know. If candidate A lists more of the keywords than candidate B, the resumes are weighted and A will receive preference," Miller says.

As another example, let's say an employer wants to fill a targeted market (Hispanic) sales position with a graduate who has majored in communications and speaks Spanish. The potential hire must live in San Antonio.

The employer might choose to search an independent resume database operated by an outside commercial firm, or an internal applicant tracking system.

In either case, the employer does keyword searching, entering the keywords that describe what the employer seeks. In this example, the keywords are *sales* (the type of position); *marketing* or *business administration* (the area of study); *Spanish* (special language skill); and *San Antonio* (geographic area).

The tracking system, using keywords, searches the database for applicants whose resumes meet these criteria. The computer displays the number of resumes that qualify. If the number is too large, the employer can add more requirements; if the number is too small, the employer can eliminate some of the required qualifications.

Suppose, for example, that a search for candidates who fit the bill yields only three resumes. The employer may decide to change the search criteria to add a willingness to relocate to San Antonio.

As a job seeker marketing yourself with a scannable resume, the most you can convey of your essence is an outline of keywords, a straightforward version of you without the grace notes of adjectives and feelings and self-serving statements.

The point about your screen image cutting to the chase is made vividly by an East Coast corporate recruiter who says, "You're naked on the screen."

MANNA FROM HEAVEN OR RESUMES FROM HELL?

Miranda Leaf (not her real name) had what most people want: a job she really enjoyed. Leaf was a contract specialist and administrative manager for a defense contractor in northern Virginia, just outside of Washington.

The problem? A new husband who lives in Southern California. "You get to the point where you realize that several thousand miles apart isn't going to work in your marriage," she says. "He was willing to relocate here, but I was tired of the winter weather anyway so I said I'd move. But where? Our lifestyle needs two incomes to support it."

Leaf spent several months mailing resumes in response to classified help-wanted ads forwarded by her new husband. Finally, she sent her resume to a company that had installed an automated applicant tracking system. At her husband's address, a call came for an interview. She was on the next plane west, to be interviewed. Within a week, she had an offer to join a major corporation within easy commuting distance from her new home. A month later, she began an attractive new job as a senior administrative manager and moved forward with her new marriage in a city where the sun almost always shines.

Leaf's easy job search via a scannable resume turned up just what she wanted. She is the model of the job seeker to whom scannable resumes are going to be the greatest thing since cellular telephones. Who are members of the group to whom scannable resumes are manna from heaven?

Almost everyone who has marketable skills and who identifies those skills largely with nouns in a computer's "vocabulary."

In the early days of electronic recruiting, conventional wisdom said that resume scanning software most benefited women, minorities, and such technical personnel as chemical engineers, computer scientists, hardware/software specialists, systems analysts, and data processors.

Today, computers, working under orders from recruiters, are zooming in on keywords to look for everyone from teachers to plumbers, from business managers to librarians.

But they aren't looking for philosophers, or other unconventional people. This is a downside of computerized resume search: The human factor seems to be missing.

When evaluating applicants, every employer needs answers to three key questions:

1. Can this person do the job?
2. Will this person do the job?
3. Will this person do the job without stressing out everyone else?

A scannable resume centered on keywords deals only with the first question: Can this person do the job?

Attitude and compatibility with the company culture can be judged in interviews, but these human factors, which can be hinted at on paper resumes, cannot be imparted electronically.

An employer may read a paper resume that says "Dependable and conscientious" or "Accurate at detail work" and be inclined to say, "Let's bring the applicant in for a look-see."

The same employer may never have the opportunity to make that judgment with an applicant tracking system because a computer generally omits human factors. A few employers will search for verbs or adjectives, but, in the main, a computer is told to talk about only proven skills and experience.

Computers are not usually urged to ask questions about interpersonal skills, motivation, drive, initiative, perseverance, resourcefulness, attitude, and cheerful outlook—or all the hundreds of other characteristics that make up a quality hire (a "dean's list" employee).

Are high-end human traits worth anything today? Of course they are; it's a matter of process. Once a pool of candidates has been identified, personal characteristics may come into play. That is, after your "skills" bring you to the surface, the human side of the resume takes over. *But first you have to get past the computer and into the pool of identified candidates.*

Let's say, for example, an automated search surfaces 21 resumes for a particular job opening. If your skills don't place you within that group of 21 candidates, you can't count on your personal characteristics to take up the skills slack and pull you into the candidates' group. You simply will never surface. When you do not surface, the human side does not have the opportunity to take over.

On a computer-scanned resume, it's difficult to find a way to make these facts *count for getting into the candidates' group:*

▶ You've worked 12-hour days to complete do-or-die assignments.

▶ You're a "versatile and analytic thinker."

▶ Others sing your praises: "My previous boss commented that I handled budgets better than anyone else in the department."

Later in the process, these fine attributes will count in selecting the winning candidate. But, as a rule, they won't bring you to the surface.

A tracking computer is a hard-nosed tool. It is interested only in provable facts, measurable quantities, and recognizable nouns, including industry jargon. It wants meat and potatoes, and prefers to skip the salad bar.

Computers, amazing as they are, still cannot come close to sorting people as effectively as human beings sort people. Although a computer functioning as part of an expert system using artificial intelligence can do a remarkable job of putting people into niches, a computer isn't creative on its own. It is programmed to behave in a predestined way.

Computers have no way to look for the unexpected. What computers expect is what they've been told to expect. Nothing more.

For job seekers with obsolete skills—or skills that do not easily convert to marketable keywords—the new scannable resume can be a horror that almost guarantees a continued state of unemployment.

A familiar example is a military service member who is trying to get out of uniform and into the job market. An enlisted service member who was trained for work in health care may be able to use as a keyword on a scannable resume the civilian job title of operating room technician and add the jargon that goes with it. One in the technical area may be able to write computer systems analyst and add a screen full of buzzwords.

Service members who were assigned to a combat specialty, however, cannot be rocketed through an applicant tracking system with such job titles as *artillery crew coordinator* or *tank gunner*. There's not much call for these in civilian society.

Aerospace defense workers who are older and have been laid off also face difficulty when they try job shopping by computer. Older engineers' records may not reflect the latest technology, as this plaintive letter shows:

> Dear Joyce:
>
> I am a BSME [mechanical engineer], 42 years old with 20 years' experience. I was laid off two years ago. Since then I have not been able to find a decent full-time job. If a company is hiring, they hire new graduates or those who obtained their degrees within the past five years. . . .

Still another group of job seekers unlikely to do well with computer-friendly resumes are liberal arts graduates without specific, identifiable skills and accomplishments. Some applicant systems are programmed to spot new graduates but, in the main, the people most wooed are those with experience—the cream of the crop.

"You've got to bring more than an appetite to the party," says James Lemke, referring to the value of skills and experience. "If you want to get invited in, bring a bottle of wine and a wheel of cheese."

For individuals on the outskirts of mainstream corporate America, the new scannables are truly resumes from hell.

THE HUMAN ISSUES CUT BOTH WAYS

Susan Ireland, a professional resume writer in North Berkeley, California, reporting in Yana Parker's *The Damn Good Resume Pro Newsletter*, is concerned about human issues:

"Resume scanning software dehumanizes the process for both the job seeker and the employer. Before the resume can be seen by a person, it first has to pass the test of a computer—a cold approach to 'human' resources.

"As resume writers, we have to be up on the terminology used in each field, or be skilled at drawing this out of our client, to be sure to use the words the employer is likely to ask for. To do that, we have to think like an employer—and think like a computer."

A leading corporate systems professional takes issue with automation being described as a "cold approach to human resources."

His rationale is that applicant tracking systems make resumes more accessible. "If every company used this type of system, there would never be a lost resume or a resume sitting in one recruiter's desk while another recruiter is out looking for a person with those skills. I agree you now need a good computer-friendly resume but at least now I will be able to find it!"

Whatever your philosophy, there's no disagreement that, in a computerized system, you play by the system's rules.

If the rules work against you, your best strategy is to stick to traditional job searches using paper resumes. You'll have a much better chance of showcasing your human condition and your potential to be a "highly competitive performer who thrives in challenging situations," or "a person who maintains a sense of humor under pressure" or is "diplomatic and assertive in dealing with people."

Looking at the brighter side of technological change, if you're a job seeker whose skills are in demand, resume databases and applicant tracking systems are a kind of tail wind that can carry you far and wide.

For one thing, the process is easy, once you've done your core scannable resume. Even if you don't use the exact job title the employer has stated, you'll still be considered for a position if you show the right mix-and-match of skills.

Surprisingly, people who might flunk a human search because of past flubs can do well in automated searches. Before making Sony one of the best known companies in the world, founder Masaru Ibuka designed a couple of "Edsels," including an electric seat warmer.

At that stage of Ibuka's career, a human recruiter might have flown right over his paper resume. A computer would have ferreted out for a second look the skills that made possible the creation of *a product*.

Later, Ibuka dreamed up the pocket-size transistor radio, the VCR, and the Walkman.

JOB HUNTING AS USUAL IS PASSÉ

Whether you are a seasoned worker at liberty, or one who is smart enough to purposefully manage your career, the time has come to update your job search skills, starting with your resume.

Even if you're a new graduate who has only recently learned how to look for a job in traditional ways, it's wise to get up to speed on the new techniques.

If you need an incentive to move off the dime and treat your job hunting and career management with the urgent priority they require, remember that the boom years following World War II are fading memories.

In the old days, with the exception of a few valleys of recession, virtually anyone with a pulse could get a job. Today's new college graduates must cope with a backlog of unhired degree holders and a surplus of their colleagues that is expected to extend into the foreseeable future. This bears repeating.

In the 1960s, jobs sought graduates; almost any bachelor's degree holder slid into a college-level job.

In the 1970s, clouds appeared. Campus recruiting dropped, and dismal headlines described college graduates who were driving cabs and waiting tables.

Hiring levels for graduates picked up again in the 1980s, but college graduates of the 1990s are finding their prospects grim—and competing with laid-off workers.

Not only will the nation's institutions of higher education turn out more graduates in the 1990–2005 period than in 1984–1990, but the jobs requiring a four-year college degree will be fewer.

Only about 70 percent of future grads are likely to find jobs requiring a college degree, compared to the longtime norm of 80 percent. *This could mean that 6 million graduates in the decade ahead will find themselves underemployed in jobs that don't require a sheepskin.*

Even after your career is successfully launched, there's no guarantee it will remain aloft. Read this letter to one of the authors.

Dear Joyce:

I have both a bachelor's and a master's degree, plus experience. I've been job hunting for seven months. I've consulted with job counselors, attended job-search workshops, and purchased books on job hunting, PMA [positive mental attitude], goal setting, and more. I have more than a dozen cassette programs by notable psychologists and inspirational motivators. I have gone bankrupt, lost my house, and lost my wife and family. I foolishly paid $15 to talk to a psychic, which tells you the near hopeless state I'm in.

We'd love to be able to tell you that the scannable resume sweeping the country is a magic bullet for all job seekers, but, unfortunately, that isn't true. Scannable resumes do, however, work wonders for job seekers who have plenty of wanted skills.

The scannable, computer-friendly resume is here to stay. For the best jobs, it will become dominant throughout the recruitment industry. The question is not "if" but "when."

Unless you're one of the people for whom scannables will never work, you must master the techniques of putting muscle into your electronic resumes—or be content to be left behind in the backwaters of the job market.

THE PERFECT TRYOUT

There's an easy and *free* way to begin to pile on expertise. Locate a library with automated search systems, and practice electronic sleuthing. You won't be searching resumes for keywords—you'll be reading whatever topics the library files electronically—but you'll learn the concept of keyword searching.

If you're feeling particularly fuzzy about the machines, don't hesitate to throw yourself on the librarian's mercy. Most librarians have turned a number of preeminent, obtuse, bumbling klutzes into confident users of the system.

Once you've mastered the electronic card catalog system, graduate to a bigger challenge. Some libraries subscribe to a database, on disk, of dozens of newspapers. Choose a topic and search—experimenting with various synonyms—until you feel comfortable with keyword searching.

Suppose you are searching for a story about minerals that supposedly increase longevity. You might look under "minerals" or "longevity" or "aging" or "health"—plus about a dozen other keywords. When a system finds a mention of one of your keywords, it's called a "hit." It's a good feeling.

The advantage you gain from practicing keyword searching is indirect but no less valuable. You condition your mind to think in terms of keywords—the concept underlying computer-friendly tracking systems.

2

The Technical Details

It Helps to Know How Scanners and OCRs Work

This chapter provides an overview of the technology that reads, stores, and retrieves resumes. It sheds light on why a good scannable resume differs from a paper resume.

Do you need to understand the finer points of how scanners and optical character recognition (OCR) software combine to process your resume? No more than you need to comprehend how a combustion engine works before you can drive a car.

But if you will take the time to absorb a smattering—just the basics—of how the technology orchestrates the flow of data through employment computers, you stand a better chance of avoiding elementary errors that can detour your paperwork.

Let's move in that direction right now with a crash tutorial.

WHAT YOU SHOULD KNOW ABOUT SCANNERS, OCRs, AND RESUMES

The scanner and its sidekick, optical character recognition software, are used throughout the world in a myriad of enterprises, from reading bank checks to reading books for the blind.

The technology has seeped into the nooks and crannies of virtually every industry. Here, we concern ourselves only with the issue at hand—*scanners and OCR software as the technology relates to your resume.*

In a nutshell, a scanner is like a photocopy machine in that it duplicates your resume and passes it on to OCR software that makes sense out of it as far as a computer is concerned.

To explain in a bit more detail, the first stop your document makes on its employment odyssey is at a scan head, the business end of a scanner.

Once a scanner has fixed its unblinking stare on your resume, the result, one might say, is digital disarray. Scanners provide only a picture of the resume—they do not give you usable text.

Like an unfinished symphony, your resume needs a few more notes before it can be widely admired by people who can hire you. It must be composed into a form appropriate for machine intelligence and that's where the OCR software makes its brilliant move. After OCR software goes to work, you have usable text that everyone can read.

More precisely, OCR software looks at a picture of a character (a letter of the alphabet) and converts it into a character of a universal computer language called ASCII (pronounced *ASkee*). ASCII is an acronym for American Standard Code for Information Interchange.

ASCII is the common text language in which most computer software programs have agreed to communicate with one another.

This computerized conversion process is called recognition—the OCR software takes the scanned images and turns them into ASCII text. In that form, the resume can be edited and sent from one system to another.

To recap, scanners record a picture of each resume on a PC. Then OCR software converts the picture into editable ASCII text. Once converted, the ASCII format can be commanded to jump through other technology hoops (word processing, spreadsheet, text retrieval, and document management applications). The result: your resume can be called up on a computer screen. Figure 2–1 summarizes the steps.

A slow scanner copies a resume page in five minutes, but a fast scanner can input a resume page in a few seconds.

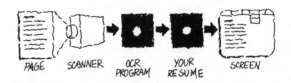

Figure 2–1   The Scanner OCR Program Process (Graphic source: Calera Recognition Systems)

THE COPY CLEANING CREW

Once information is copied and sent into a computer, a clerk—often called a verifier/operator—reviews the on-screen form to ensure that it matches the printed resume. Any corrections needed are made at this stage.

The marvelous OCR software gets better every year but is not letter-perfect. The characters may become "degraded," or squashed. Degraded text is examined in Chapter 4, but Figure 2–2 previews the assortment of characters with which OCR programs wrestle.

Understandably, OCR software at times garbles words, making them appear to be misspelled. Washed-out resumes or resumes with unusual typefaces may not decode correctly. This is how one system scanned in error:

REFERENCES (Southern Ckifomia clients and other influential con-tacts) Italian Leatlzer Accessories, Ci-oce's Restaurant, Hollywood ilverkorks, Hoilon Plaza Fanners Market.

We assume this translates to:

REFERENCES (Southern California clients and other influential contacts): Italian Leather Accessories, Ciro's Restaurant, Hollywood Silverworks, Horton Plaza Farmers Market.

A text cleanup by a human crew doesn't take long. Operator/verifiers are told to do it as quickly as possible. In fact, some cost-conscious companies instruct their scanner clerks not to edit insignificant details or experience that's older than five years. (For older workers, this money-saving practice is very good news; it ex-pands their inclusion in the first cut of candidates for a job.)

Some companies verify only the name and contact information on the resumes, declining to clean up the text at all. They believe it

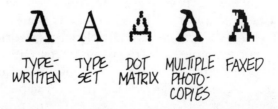

Figure 2–2   **Characters OCR Software Scans (Graphic source: Calera Recognition Systems)**

isn't worth the expense. The practice of cleaning up text is likely to virtually disappear over the next few years because it is the most labor-intensive part of the process, and because scanning recognition technology is continually improving.

HOW YOUR RESUME IS VIEWED

Depending on the tracking system the hiring employer is using, your resume can be reviewed in one, two, or all three of these basic forms:

1. An exact picture of the original resume (or standardized application form). An image of the original document allows hiring managers to see whether a resume is attractively laid out and whether it contains spelling errors. It offers a glimpse of the person behind the resume. This kind of additional information can have a definite impact on a hiring decision.
2. The full text of the resume, which is engineered to match closely the look of the original resume; however, all items may be presented in linear, flush-left form.
3. An applicant summary, also called an extracted summary, a qualifications summary, or a qualifications brief. An example of this abbreviated document appears in Chapter 3.

Employers sensitive to antidiscrimination law do not refer to an individual as an applicant until that person is routed to a hiring manager. Until then, the individual is an "inquirer." These employers tend to call the capsules of people who have inquired about working for them "extracted summaries" or "qualifications summaries."

Many other employers simply call the identical documents "applicant summaries."

By any name, this piece of information is a capsule. In outline form, it contains your name and address, telephone number, degrees, work history (dates, companies, job titles), key skill, and experience descriptions. The summary is marked with job coding that can classify a resume in multiple job categories.

For example, a software engineer with technical writing and marketing experience would automatically qualify for four job categories, rather than just one. This professional would be filed in the categories of "software engineering," "technical writing," "sales engineering," and "marketing."

OCR SYSTEMS ARE NOT THE SAME

The OCR systems now available offer vastly different capabilities. One important difference is their ability to read type correctly, that is, to recognize fonts.

In case you've forgotten, a font is a collection of letters and other characters, all within the same typeface and all of the same size. Courier, for instance, is the name of a popular typeface. Courier 10 point, Courier Bold 12 point, and Courier Italic 10 point are three separate fonts.

This is Courier 10 point.

This is Courier Bold 12 point.

This is Courier Italic 10 point.

The font sophistication of OCR systems can be broadly grouped into the following three categories.

1. Polyfont recognition. Polyfont OCR can read a limited number of fonts. Many polyfont software programs will recognize only specific fonts and cannot recognize others.

   Your resume may cross paths with a polyfont OCR system that never heard of the relatively uncommon fonts you've chosen; if so, never the twain shall communicate. Stick with familiar typefaces.

2. Trainable recognition. You can teach a trainable OCR system to recognize virtually any font that comes along.

   Each font and style, however, requires extensive learning sessions for workers—another reason why you should stick with tried-and-true typefaces.

3. Omnifont recognition. These systems, the high end of the OCR market, can recognize virtually any font that maintains fairly standard character shapes.

   True omnifont systems require no training or other adjustments to accommodate different fonts. Omnifont recognition rapidly is becoming the standard for systems used in the human resource arena, but you still can't count on your resume encountering it.

By now you've deduced why all this information is important to you as a job seeker. OCR scanners do make mistakes. In the technical world, it's called the degree of "recognition accuracy" (or lack thereof).

Recognition accuracy measures how many characters (letters) are incorrectly recognized on a given page. For example, on a typical 2,000-character resume page, 98 percent accuracy means 40 errors—up to 40 letters may have been misread. A 99 percent accuracy rate means 20 errors.

We've shared this cautionary tale of potential technical follies to emphasize how necessary it is to assemble a solid and scannable resume that can be read by a fussy machine. Chapter 4 takes you further along this path of knowledge.

A TYPICAL TRIP THROUGH THE "TRACKER"

After a name goes into a database, the system usually is told to generate a thank-you letter to the applicant. It's almost wand-waving-easy to post hundreds of letters daily.

When a job requisition comes into a human resource office, a hiring manager tells a recruiter which requirements the applicants *must* meet.

Usually there are three levels of criteria: (1) "must haves," (2) "desirables," and (3) "nice if you can get them." Sometimes only the first two levels—"must haves" and "desirables"—are listed.

The recruiter heads for a mouse or keyboard and searches the database, using keywords.

Figure 2–3 illustrates the process flow of one system, Resumix.

A computer displays the number of resumes that meet the required criteria. Too many? The recruiter can fine-tune (add, enhance, change) the requirements. Too few? The recruiter can adjust the requirements in the opposite direction.

Once the system comes up with the right number of applicants, the recruiter can take a look at the resumes or resume summaries (also called applicant summaries or extracted summaries) and, after human inspection, send back any that aren't suitable for the job opening.

Next, the recruiter can order the system to print specified resumes. The printouts may be exact copies of the original resumes, or they may appear in a standardized resume format, more like an application form.

The hard copies can be mailed to the hiring managers, or the system can ferry the resumes over e-mail or the fax line.

This means your resume can be, as Restrac executives put it, in two places—or in 200 places—at once.

The operation of the Hewlett-Packard Employment Response Center in Palo Alto, California, illustrates how a resume can be

RESUME PROCESSING WITH RESUMIX

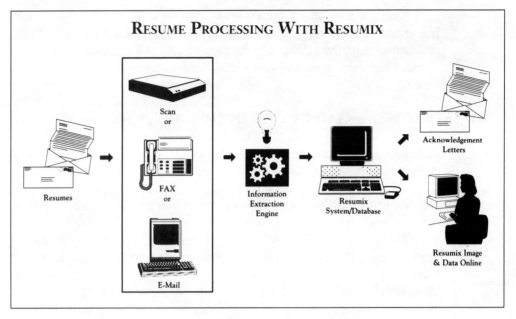

Figure 2–3   Resumix Flow Chart

everywhere at once. Hewlett-Packard Company (HP) operates an enterprisewide, automated employment management system using Restrac technology.

When a resume is scanned into the system, the pertinent facts are extracted and the document is stored as a qualifications summary along with the reformatted resume and the cover letter, explains Michelle Greer, HP's staffing programs manager.

"Our system makes it possible for every HP manager in the United States to easily see your information. The cover letters are especially useful because it is here that applicants are encouraged to tell us their geographic and job preferences," says Greer.

Multidistribution of resumes is a strong feature of this technology. Every authorized person gets to see a resume, not just the person who saw it first and filed it in a desk somewhere.

"Your information will be reviewed every time an HP manager has a job requisition appropriate to your background and interests. When a manager sees that your qualifications fit a job opening, he or she will call you," Greer explains.

Greer adds that applicants in their database may receive telephone calls from more than one interested manager with a job opening. If no appropriate job openings are available after six months, your records are placed into electronic archives unless you ask the Employment Response Center to keep you in the active files.

Don't worry about your name and personal information floating around across the nation. Unlike a simple computer file that anyone can access, the HP system has a security system that allows only authorized managers to have access to the resumes.

THE LATEST BREAKTHROUGHS IN OCR SYSTEMS

Among industry leaders marketing OCR software today are these companies: Caere Corporation, Calera Recognition Systems, Inc., Cognitive Technology Corporation, CTA, Inc., ExperVision, Inc., OCRON, Inc., Recognita Corporation of America, and Xerox Imaging Systems, Inc.

The earliest version of what commonly is known today as OCR appeared in 1959. Developed by the Intelligent Machine Research Corporation, the first commercial page reader boasted a scanner and OCR software that could read one font in one point size.

This inspired but humble beginning led to systems that could read many fonts. In 1978, Kurzweil Computer Products (now Xerox Imaging Systems, Inc.) produced a system that could be user-trained to read any given font. It took several hours of instruction per font, but it led to further refinements.

Most OCR systems of the late 1970s and early 1980s used the rule-based methods of artificial intelligence. The technology works well for many fonts on clean pages, but is less impressive on less pristine pages.

The machine vision industry really left the launching pad in 1986 when Calera Recognition Systems, Inc., introduced omnifont recognition technology. It works through a machine-learning technique that mimics human learning and is known as "neural networks."

In neural networks, a computer is able to recognize typefaces it has never encountered by drawing clues from the characters. It compares those clues with the information it has already learned. Like an electronic Sherlock Holmes, the OCR can then make a generalization (deduction or good guess) about the new typeface.

That was good progress, but now the technology is moving from gee-whiz to whiz-bang in document reading. One example is what Calera calls Adaptive Recognition Technology. Introduced in 1993, this advanced technology works like a crew of crack code-breakers deciphering text in which the characters are trashed and almost illegible.

As a for-instance, Calera's new dynamic information technology compensates for such effects as black lines running down a page and obscuring words (caused by malfunctioning photocopiers), or the mystery holes left when faxes drop lines.

ExperVision, Inc. and Xerox Imaging Systems, Inc., also are reported to have advanced programs for salvaging degraded text. Others are sure to follow.

Even Adaptive Recognition Technology isn't the end of the machine-reading rainbow. On the horizon are software programs harnessing new technology that removes elements offensive to scanning systems, such as underlining and italic text. Even if you put the criminal elements in, these smarty-pants programs yank them right out of your resume. *Poof!* They're gone! The process may cut off a few characters at the knees, but, in the name of scannability, your resume can live with that. The problem is that several years, at a minimum, will pass before these "scanfixing" programs are widely in use.

When you realize the enormous leaps forward made by scanning and OCR technology during the past decade, you have a firm inkling of the changes yet to come and of how increasing automation will affect the way you and your children find jobs.

HOW SMART PROGRAMS WORK THE CROWD

Some applicant tracking systems take snapshots of both your resume data and your original resume and electronically store them for future searches. Often, your cover letter goes into the electronic cupboard as well. Glance at the Restrac system shown in Figure 2–4.

By contrast, other trackers store only the resume data, usually in the form of an extracted summary or standardized resume form, and do not include a picture of the original document.

As a job seeker, you have no control over which types of systems guard your resume. The first option does more for you than the second. Shoehorning you into a one-size-fits-all format does little to illustrate the essence of your individuality.

Once the document is scanned into the system, the retrieval software takes over. Here, one more great divide among systems becomes apparent.

The available software can take one of three approaches:

1. Electronic/Manual coding systems.
2. Total recall systems (a.k.a. total recall with perfect precision or full text, free form search retrieval systems). We can nickname them "total recall" or "free form" search.

3. Knowledge-based systems or, more formally, artificial intelligence knowledge-based expert systems.

As in the ongoing debate about which personal computers are superior, IBM PCs or Macintosh PCs, each of these types of systems has its partisans.

From the job seeker's viewpoint, the second and third types of software offer notable advantages.

Electronic/Manual Coding Systems

First-generation applicant tracking systems are electronic counterparts of manual coding systems. Working from a scheme of predefined categories, data entry clerks code each resume as it comes in, and then send it off to the appropriate electronic filing drawer. Manual skill coding, because of the labor costs and risk of mistakes in

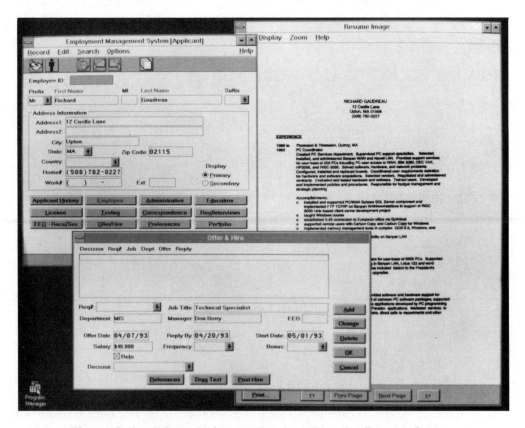

Figure 2–4   A Sample Screen Produced by the Restrac System

categorizing resumes, is considered by many human resource professionals to be a declining approach.

Total Recall Systems

Resumes entering these systems are, figuratively speaking, placed in a large electronic storeroom. They are kept in random order, not sorted by occupation.

Advocates of this type of system believe skill coding is extremely subjective. They argue that two manual coders can read a resume of an individual with a divergent background and come to different conclusions on how to code or classify the individual.

Once a skill is assigned and the resume is sent off to its electronic home, other pertinent skills or expertise—not identified in the initial evaluation—are not readily retrievable, according to total recall proponents.

A total recall search can find in a database any applicant whose resume reflects the words or series of words supplied by the employer. Without a predefined knowledge base to limit the search, anything or any word is fair game.

Think of tracking hounds being imprinted with the scent of a wanted person and let loose to pursue that person no matter where the trail leads, and you've grasped the main idea of a total recall system.

All of your resume contents, 100 percent, are automatically entered into the system's search dictionary. If an employer wants anything on your resume, it's there. The database owned by a particular employer contains only the information fed into it by that employer. Because the employer created it, the database is proprietary.

Some total recall systems offer a feature favorable to job seekers: force feeding of the total resume. After an employer completes a search, the entire text of the appropriate resume is displayed on the screen with all matching keywords highlighted.

If you're on the short list, the recruiter is compelled to see the image of your full resume, which is a very good thing for you. Once your resume is on the screen, the recruiter's eyes may be drawn to other compelling facts about you that were not in the keyword search. This happy turn of events may reinforce a decision to issue an interview invitation.

Proponents of total recall systems believe they well serve job seekers in certain occupations. Sales is an example.

As a systems manager of a giant corporation explains, "Sales people don't have resumes that are noun-based. They say things like

'I sold $100,000 worth of stuff.' A total recall system is excellent to search not only for 'things,' but for subjective words as well."

Knowledge-Based Systems

Referring back to the metaphor of the tracking hounds, in a knowledge-based system the trackers are steered in a particular direction: "Head north and bear to the west; the wanted person is hiding out in an electronic filing cabinet in the Northwest sector."

The trackers are pointed in the right direction because this type of system uses artificial intelligence to code the skills on your resume, pinpointing job and industry classifications.

You may be classified in as many as six occupational clusters, and your applicant summary may be stored in as many as six appropriate electronic filing cabinets. (You send only one copy of your resume; it is electronically replicated.)

Job classification is general; sample headings are "software engineer" and "clerical." Jobs you never thought about may come your way if your skills fill the bill.

How are the classifications determined? By every piece of information extracted from the resume by the knowledge-based systems. Skills, job titles, majors, degrees, schools, and companies—all communicate information about the industry and help to assign the job classification appropriate for the resume.

Based on a word database—known as a "knowledge base"— this type of system offers a vast number of synonyms and keywords. To code in the same set of skills that the system finds automatically, a data-entry clerk would need fairly sophisticated knowledge of the different industry areas covered by the knowledge base.

Knowing, for instance, that Aix and Posix both imply a computer system known as Unix is beyond the kind of expertise a data-entry clerk is expected to have.

As a job seeker, this category of system offers you the advantage of more flexibility in the words you choose. The knowledge base is likely to figure out that even if your word isn't exactly the same as one the search engine is tracking, a rose is a rose is a rose. (A fuller explanation of this point is found in Chapter 4.)

The knowledge-based systems cull their expertise from hundreds of recruiters; hence the term "expert system." With an expert system, data-entry personnel don't need a high level of synonym expertise.

People who love words, such as clever author Paul Dickson (*Dickson's Word Treasury: A Connoisseur's Collection of Old and New,*

Weird and Wonderful, Useful and Outlandish Words) may enjoy exploring this whole new world of synonymy.

NO TURNING BACK

Quietly but quickly, resume scanning and applicant tracking systems are making their mark. Old methods are becoming obsolete as each day passes.

Any chance of turning back the clock to the days when all human resource professionals and recruiters manually sorted through resumes, read them, interpreted what they contained, and struggled to code them for retrieval later? We don't think so. The old way is too time-consuming and expensive.

Holding back change driven by cost-effectiveness is like trying to hold back a rushing river with a worn-out dam. Bet on the river.

3

Key Concepts for Keywords

How You Can Use Labels to Manage the Perils of High-Speed Searching

This chapter helps develop your keyword skills. The concept is unfamiliar to most people, but it is becoming critical to a successful job search.

As you saw in the previous chapter, employers are choreographing the recruitment process with scanning and recognition technology.

The most qualified candidates come center-screen on hiring companies' computers. Second-tier candidates land in the understudy ranks, ready in case the stars conk out. The candidates who are near-misses never make it to the screen at all.

The scanning/OCR technology described in the preceding chapter is used in both resume databases of corporate internal applicant tracking systems, and in independent resume databases to which employers turn.

Your challenge is to avoid being passed over—to find a way to coax your name out of the computer vaults of the trackers.

You can minimize the risk of being passed over, but it will take a dose of rethinking how you present yourself on a resume. You've got some unlearning to do.

From your student days, can you recall a stream of teachers warning you of the insensitivity you display when you label people?

Don't put labels on people. The wrong label grinds a person down, lowering that person's self-esteem. Labeling is judging a person before you get to know that person. Just because a person is short . . . fat . . . tall . . . thin, it doesn't mean . . . .

Your kindergarten teacher told you labeling isn't a nice thing to do. Your elementary grade teachers insisted you can't tell a book by its cover. Your high school social science teachers warned that earmarking people is politically incorrect.

Because your teachers along your entire education ladder added their condemnation of the human tendency to put tags on people, by twelfth grade you had gotten the message that labeling is unacceptable in polite society.

Labeling prejudges. It encourages bigotry. It creates stereotypes. It is unfair. It wreaks havoc in the civilized world.

If these messages took root, you probably haven't consciously thought much about labeling since then. Avoiding thoughtless classification of other people is still a good idea, but the time has come to revise your attitudes about **labeling yourself**. As a job seeker, the time has come to shift gears and think of yourself in terms of labels.

In a contemporary job search, you must think about labels each time you write a resume or tailor your core resume for a specific position.

What's the reason for chucking remnants of what you learned in school about labeling? **The technology responsible for computer-readable resumes operates on the principle of labeling**. At the center of the technology are keywords. Call them buzzwords. Call them descriptors. Call them skills words, or job words. Call them whatever you like—labeling is labeling.

KEYWORDS MARK THE SEARCH TRAIL

When an employer sends a job requisition through an applicant tracking system, the light at the end of the electronic pathway falls on well-defined labels of the women and men most suitable for the position.

Let's take as an example a recent job order for an account executive in directory publishing. By analyzing the job order, we see the labels the employer requires:

▸ A five-years'-experience salesperson.
▸ A college graduate.

▶ A direct marketer to ethnic communities.

▶ A heavy traveler.

▶ A self-starter.

▶ A team leader.

All these requirements are labels that mark the electronic trail followed by recruiters.

Supplied with these keywords, a computer races along across the hills and individuals dales of a resume database until it comes up with the individuals best matched to the labels.

Each time a computer makes a decision that either makes your screen presence felt or leaves you in the electronic dark, it is making judgment calls on the basis of labels. The secret to screen stardom in computerized job searches is to put as many labels as possible on your resume. Feed the system all the labels it wants, here, there, and everywhere.

In real estate, the three important words are "location, location, location." In the resume revolution, the three important words are "labels, labels, labels."

When you're in the job market, you must overcome all your inhibitions about *labeling yourself*. Forget shyness and forget modesty. Label yourself. That's what the keyword concept is about.

TWO EXAMPLES OF KEYWORD SEARCHING

The telecommunications industry is now bigger than computers or aerospace, according to Columbia University's Center for Telecommunications and Information Studies. A stream of innovative products—electronic data networks, information services, long-distance packages, cellular car telephones, and fax—has caused telephone usage to grow almost three times as fast as the population.

Bell Atlantic in Arlington, Virginia, is the "Baby Bell" company serving the Mid-Atlantic region, including the nation's capital.

Realizing that Bell Atlantic has state-of-the-art technology, we asked Jane Paradiso, the information company's director of human resource service systems, to create fictional illustrations of how specific job requisitions would move through Bell Atlantic's automated applicant tracking system.

Using a dialogue of co-author Tom Morrow's questions and Jane Paradiso's comments, here are two illustrations. The first is for a professional job; the second, for a clerical position.

Overseas Accountant

Morrow: Where will the person chosen for this position work?

Paradiso: In this illustration, we are staffing a financial position in Czechoslovakia where an accountant with public experience is required. This is what the job requisition looks like:

Job Requisition for Overseas Accountant

Required Buzzword: Accounting

Required Degree: BA

Required Major: Finance

Desired Buzzword: Cost Accounting   Public Accounting
                     Acct'ing Principles   Financial Status
                     Account Analysis   Corp Financial Sys
                     Revenue Accounting   Quality Programs
                     CPA   Leadership   Czech   French

Desired Company: Arthur Andersen
                     Coopers & Lybrand
                     Deloitte & Touche
                     Ernst & Young
                     KPMG Peat Marwick
                     Price Waterhouse

Morrow: The *required* buzzwords, *degree* and *major,* are pretty clear. Can you comment on the *desired* buzzwords?

Paradiso: First, notice that they are not action verbs, but nouns. In computer-read resumes, action verbs are virtually obsolete. Nouns that state specific skills—Unix [a computer system], TQM [total quality management], and leadership, for instance—are the best kinds of words to guarantee selection. Desired buzzwords [keywords] mean just that—we prefer that a candidate have these qualifications but each one is not essential. The candidates with the greatest number of desired buzzwords—plus desired company experience—will rise to the top of the short list.

Here are four resumes. Look them over and see how many of the required and desired buzzwords you can find in each of them. A computer, of course, can do it in a flash.

LEONARD J. MALIK

1485 Norton Court
North Vancouver
Canada, V7G 2ES

CHARTERED ACCOUNTANT
B.C. Residence: (604) 929-0422
Message: (604) 663-3278

EDUCATION

1985 Chartered Accountant (C.A.)

1982 Bachelor of Commerce (Accounting and Finance)
University of Toronto

CAREER HISTORY:

Feb 1990 - Present
Revenue Accounting Manager
B.C. Telephone Company, Burnaby, B.C.

B.C. Tel. is one of the largest telecommunications companies in
Canada which, with its subsidiaries, is engaged in basic
telephone service, advanced voice and data equipment and
services, research and development, information management,
consulting, financial services, equipment manufacturing and
maintenance, and wireless communications.

As Revenue Accounting Manager, I am accountable for all Revenue
Reporting, Revenue Settlement and Cash Control functions. Revenue
Accounting is the focal point for all revenue analysis and toll
forecasting, while Revenue Settlement reports and settles toll
revenues with other domestic and foreign telephone companies.
Cash control is the audit center for cash processing. I am also
responsible for the implementation of a new Revenue Accounting
Information System.

Feb 1988 - Feb 1990
Accounting Supervisor
Strategic Planning and Financial Analysis Department
B.C. Tel. (Business Telecom Equipment Division), Burnaby, B.C.

I was responsible for the preparation of the five year strategic
plan, annual detailed budget, and monitoring and analysis of
variances. Also responsible for implementing and coordinating
yearly inventory counts and other special projects.

Sept 1986 - Feb 1988
Controller
Cendix Avelex Inc. (Aaro-Marine Division), Richmond, B.C.

Cendix Avelex is a unit of the Rally-Signal Aerospace Sector of
Rally-Signal Corp., a major innovator in aerospace and marine
technology. Its marine subdivision is a sales and distribution
agent for a Japanese marine equipment manufacturer.

As Controller (promoted from Accounting Supervisor), I was
responsible for the implementation of internal controls,
preparation of monthly financial statements, and day-to-day
accounting, credit, and collection functions.

July 1985 - Sept 1986
Chief Accountant
Tall & Redekop Corporation, Vancouver, B.C.

Tall & Radekop is a real estate company involved in construction,
land development, and property management.

Reporting directly to the Chairman of the Board, I was
responsible for the preparation of consolidated financial
statements, financial and management reporting of all the
divisions, computerization of manual financial records and the
daily financing and investing activities of the corporation. In
addition, responsible for the supervision of all accounting and
support staff.

June 1982 - July 1985
Audit Senior
Price Waterhouse Chartered Accountants, Vancouver, B.C.

As Audit Senior, I was responsible for the planning and execution
of professional services to clients ranging from charitable
organizations to public utilities and multinational forest
products companies.

HONORS, ACHIEVEMENTS

1983 Ranked within the top 15% on the Chartered Accountants
qualifying examination.

1976 High school treasurer and member of the student council.

Marital Status Married
Place of Birth: Czechoslovakia   Languages: English, Czech

Kenneth L. Garnet

6430 SW 126th Street
Miami, FL 33126-5568
(305) 665-1994

Objective: To use proven problem-solving and profit improvement skills as a Controller or in Senior Management of Finance, Accounting, Purchasing, and/or Information Systems.

SUMMARY: Florida CPA with 19 years of progressively more responsible management positions in information systems, accounting, and purchasing. Experience includes management of: administrative purchasing, purchasing and accounting controls and procedures, operational accounting and analysis, and major information system implementations. Managed staff of 25 to 50 with budgets of $3 million. Achieved cost savings conservatively estimated at more than $20 million.

PROFESSIONAL EXPERIENCE

RYDER SYSTEMS, INC., Miami, FL   September 1978 to Present: Director, Purchasing Administration.

Controller of $1 billion purchasing operation. Also responsible for purchasing of administrative goods and services.

* Established a captive vehicle dealer, resulting in sales tax savings of over $800,000 annually.
* Negotiated a preferred supplier relationship with a single major carrier for all travel in and out of Miami, which will save more than $200,000 annually in air travel costs by concentrating travel with a single airline.
* Instituted a complete analysis of the vehicle order cycle process, eliminating paperwork delays and conducting feedback sessions and suppliers on their performance. Delivery cycle was shortened to 120 days, reducing cost by $9 million annually.
* Designed and implemented new system to evaluate 500 field locations' participating in centrally negotiated purchasing programs. Increased usage of the programs resulted in purchase savings of $1 million annually.

Assistant Controller, Vehicle Administration

Controller responsible for asset management of 150,000-vehicle fleet.

* Conducted extensive review of vehicle depreciation policy, implemented significant changes to lease pricing factors,

improving sales force focus on most profitable vehicle types.
Negotiated terms and conditions, and established administrative
controls, for a 600-tractor, $36 million operating lease
contract.

Director, Insurance Accounting

Controller responsible for liability, physical damage, and
workers' compensation insurance programs for $2.5 billion vehicle
leasing and rental business.

* Developed comprehensive review and analysis of $100 million
  insurance product line.
* Established new reporting systems for field operating
  management rating their performance in workers' compensation
  and highway accident frequency. Reduced accidents in both
  categories by 10 percent over one-year period.

Director, MIS Technology

Responsible for planning, evaluating, designing, and implementing
computer-based technology for $2.5 billion division. Managed
technical staff responsible for telecommunications, system
software, hardware and software planning, and office automation.

* Conducted review and technical evaluation of mini-computer
  alternatives for automating field office, resulting in Board
  of Directors approval for $30 million, 5-year project with
  estimated savings of $5 million annually.

Productivity Task Force (special assignment)

Conducted comprehensive quality program, soliciting and
evaluating over 3,000 suggestions from company field
organization.

Group Project Manager/Project Manager

Increasingly responsible application development management
positions for financial and personnel systems.

* Completed a number of significant applications projects in the
  financial and human resources area, including accounts
  payable, human resources, and general ledger upgrades.

COOPERS & LYBRAND, New York, NY,   June 1972 to September 1978

Systems Analyst

* On team for IBM database project in Pala Corporation,
   developing a worldwide financial reporting system.

PRICE WATERHOUSE, New York, NY, June 1968 to September 1971

Systems Analyst

* Supervised communications equipment for the Paris peace talks,
   and helped set up the communications center for the first
   strategic arms limitation talks in Vienna.

PROFESSIONAL/EDUCATION

Certified Public Accountant, Florida; Member AICPA, FICPA, Passed
CPA exam in May 1982. Obtained highest grade in the State of
Florida, also received Elija Watt Sells Award as one of the 103
highest grades of 65,000 individuals who took the examination.

University of Pennsylvania, Wharton School, M.B.A., 1972.
Major: Corporate Finance, Information Systems Option
Rank: Top 25% of class

Yale University, B.S. 1968
Major: Engineering and Applied Science (Electrical)
Chairman, Yale Scientific Magazine

Exchange Student in Paris for junior year in high school. Fluent
in French.

JACK T. TONY
1142 Soldiers Field Park #606
Chicago, IL 66666
(312) 566-8812

Harvard Graduate. School of Business Administration. Boston.
Master in Business Administration. Publisher. Harbus News.
University of Cincinnati. Bachelor's of Business Administration.
Summa Cum Laude. Finance. Accounting. Outstanding Student Award.
Omicron Delta Kappa. Beta Gamma Sigma. Student Body President.
Associate. Chief Executive. Problem Solving. Financial Analyst.

Educational Experience:

HARVARD GRADUATE SCHOOL OF BUSINESS ADMINISTRATION Boston, MA
Master in Business Administration degree, 1993.
Publisher, The Harbus News. Responsible for managing operations
of weekly campus newspaper.

UNIVERSITY OF CINCINNATI, Cincinnati, Ohio
Bachelor of Business Administration degree, summa cum laude,
double major in Finance and Accounting 1989.
Received College of Business Administration Outstanding Student
Award.
Delivered commencement oration to 12,000 guests.
Omicron Delta Kappa, Beta Gamma Sigma, Golden Key and Mortar
Board honoraries.
Student Body President: Represented 35,000 students.
Chief Executive of Student Government office.

Professional Experience:

BOOM FINANCIAL CONSULTING, Philadelphia, PA
1992 Summer Associate.
Member of a team which assisted senior management in the
publishing division of a major information services company. Led
the team in problem-solving for several key areas: Evaluated the
firm's cost structure, analyzed the economics of their industry
and identified opportunities in monitoring and improving the
marketing and sales functions.

BOOM FINANCIAL CORPORATION, Cleveland, Ohio
1989-1991
Assistant to the Chairman and Financial Analyst. Provided a wide
range of services and problem solving as support staff for
chairman and chief executive officer of this $8 billion private
diversified holding company and its subsidiaries.

RHONDA LOCOCO
1020 N. Lake Shore Drive, Apt. 1505-N
Chicago, IL 60615
(312) 224-7655

SUMMARY

Licensed Certified Public Accountant with more than three years'
experience as a senior associate in a major accounting firm.
Offering client management and auditing skills.

EDUCATION

BOSTON COLLEGE, BS degree in Accounting, Finance 1989
GPA: Overall 3.75; Majors 3.92; Summa Cum Laude, member Beta
Gamma Sigma, Alpha Sigma Nu

EXPERIENCE

ANSEL REED & Company, Boston

April 1989 to Present
Senior Associate

Reviewed SEC writings and participated in audits of financial
systems and reports, bond exchanges. Developed and implemented
engagement strategies. Coordinated audit and client management
and administered audit fieldwork. Prepared and analyzed financial
statements and annual reports. Exposed to a wide variety of
industries including health care, hi-tech and electronics
manufacturing, retail, and software.

PROFESSIONAL ACTIVITIES/ACHIEVEMENTS

* Awarded AICPA's Elijah Watt Sells Award for performance with
  high distinction.
* Scored in the top 100 for CPA examination for candidates in
  the U.S.
* Member of Massachusetts Society of CPAs.
* Proficient in DOS, Lotus 1-2-3, Windows, WordPerfect, Excel,
  and dBase VI.

Morrow: Which candidate crossed the finish line first?

Paradiso: Here's the short list. A rating of three points is the highest score, meaning Kenneth Garnet came in first, followed by Leonard Malik. Rhonda Lacoco rated one point. Jack Tony is in a group with no points.

Ranking of Candidates for Overseas Accountant Position

<< 3 >>
GARNET, Kenneth L.

<< 2 >>
MALIK, Leonard J.

<< 1 >>

LOCOCO, Rhonda	BRIGHT, Cal	CHOSKI, Sapna
DIXON, Helene	BITTEL, Roger	KIM, Joon
KORMAN, J.	BONDA, Andy	REES, Petra
RIM, James	ROSS, James	WILLIAM J. SC

<< 0 >>

RANAPOLSKY, Jos	AUKERMAN, Don	BUTMAN, Mark
TONY, Jack T.	DAWSON, Ken	FRIEND, Sally
GEGER, Patty	LEREN, Rodney	WICKS, Melvin
BOPKINS, Bob	JACKSON, Grant	HETTE, Tonya
KLERK, Cynthia	LEE, Robert	LEDBETTER, Mitch
LEIDNER, Mitch	CLARK-IVY, Pat	LOY, Patrick
LOPEZ, Juan	LUT, Daniel	MANDELL, Barb
NOWAK, George	OGILVIE, David	PLANT, Jerry
QUATTRO, Dean	RALLO-RENDUGO, K.	RITZON, Mary
SLOAN, Peter	SPRINGLER, Tim	STEFANI, Tiffany
WALKER, Paul	WHITE, Steven	

Morrow: Can you elaborate on this result, Jane?

Paradiso: The job requisition *requires* that all candidates have a BA in finance, as well as accounting experience. Therefore, the computer first found all candidates in the database with these requirements. Additionally, the computer looked for desired skills and experience in *desired* companies. Candidate Kenneth Garnet has three of the desired buzzwords. Leonard Malik has two. Rhonda Lococo has one. Jack Tony has only the required skills. Kenneth Garnet has all the required skills plus three of the desired skills* (CPA, Coopers & Lybrand, Price Waterhouse).

*In human resource circles, "skills" is sometimes used as an all-inclusive term that also means experience, previous blue-chip employers, and other attributes.

Leonard Malik has all the required skills, but only two desired skills and experience (Czech and Price Waterhouse). Rhonda Lococo has one desired skill (French).

Morrow: Does this mean Kenneth Garnet gets the job?

Paradiso: Not necessarily. In a normal environment, the hiring manager or recruiter would scan the top candidates, probably first looking at Garnet, then Malik, Lococo, and so forth. The specifics on their resumes would be reviewed, and management judgment would be utilized to decide which candidates to interview. The computer system is used to screen and select the best candidates, those with the largest number of desired skills, in addition to those meeting all requirements. After that, human judgment takes over.

Receptionist/Secretary

Morrow: Is this job overseas too?

Paradiso: No, it's in a domestic Bell Atlantic office. This is a clerical position. The person hired will deal both with English- and Spanish-speaking customers. Requirements are for experience as a secretary, fluency in Spanish, and skill with WordPerfect. Additionally, experience in answering telephones, personal computer literacy, and student personnel work would be helpful. Here's the job requisition:

Job Requisition for Receptionist/Secretary

Required Buzzword:	Secretarial WordPerfect Spanish
Desired Category:	General
Desired Buzzword:	Personal Computer Phones Student Personnel

Morrow: This looks straightforward. What happens next?

Paradiso: Let's look at four resumes for this clerical opening—as the computer would see them. Look for buzzwords.

SARAH JO DOLAN
2782 Mountain View Rd.
Newark, NJ 07000
(201) 334-9007

Objective: Administrative/Secretarial Position

Summary: Goal-oriented administrative professional with extensive clerical and office experience. Fluent in Spanish. Skills in:

* WordPerfect 6.0   * Digital VT 220
* Dictaphone   * LOTUS
* IBM-PC   * Macintosh

Professional Experience:

ABC BENEFIT SERVICES, Jersey City, NJ -- 1990 to 1991

Administrative Assistant

Prepared monthly billing invoices. Controlled payment of vendor invoices. Prepared status report for monthly processing. Updated participant's addresses and location codes. Purchased office supplies and maintained operational equipment.

YANKEE DOODLE, Inc., Weehawken, NJ -- 1989 to 1990

Administrative Assistant

Promoted to full time. Maintained account documents and client files. Prepared distributions for profit sharing plans. Processed contributions for employee pension plans.

Word Processor

Typed and edited internal audit reports.

THOMASON REALTY CO., North Bergen, NJ -- 1986 to 1988

Office Manager

Light bookkeeping. Set up business meetings. Processed vendor invoices. Responsible for business accounts. Heavy phone work, filing, word processing.

CANINE WESTMINSTER BANK, Hoboken, NJ -- 1984 to 1986

Secretary

CRT operation. Administrative duties. Heavy customer service work. Telephone interaction with clients. Opened and processed new bank accounts.

Education:

ST. FRANCIS COLLEGE, Jersey City, NJ, 1989
Accounting Major -- 6 credits with 3.25 average

PERRY SCHOOL FOR EXECUTIVE SECRETARIES,
Newark, NJ 1981 to 1982
Certificate in Secretarial Studies with an A average.

SHARON BULLOCK
335 Canyon Lane
Chicago, IL 99979
(312) 678-0907

PROFESSIONAL EXPERIENCE

December 1986 to August 1992 -- FT. KNOX BANK, Philadelphia
Staff Specialist, Trust Department, Employee Benefit Sales Group.

* Coordinated marketing materials for sales meetings and
  mailings. Compiled monthly and quarterly new business reports.
* Acted as translator at numerous employee benefit seminars held
  by bank customers to explain to their Spanish-speaking
  employees 401(k) and/or profit-sharing plans.
* Processed contributions and checks for large pension accounts.
* Performed administrative and secretarial duties.

May 1981 to December 1986 -- FT. KNOX BANK, Philadelphia
Head Teller

* Responsible for the operation of the teller section of the
  branch.
* Assisted customers with various transactions; settled bank
  statements; opened and closed accounts; issued money orders,
  travelers checks, and bank checks.
* Prepared monthly audit reports.
* Responsible for the branch's Automatic Teller Machine.

August 1979 to March 1981 -- SECOND HAWAIIAN BANK,
Honolulu, HI
Teller

* Assisted customers with various transactions; opened and
  closed accounts, issued money orders, travelers checks and
  bank checks.
* Used CRT to process customer deposits and withdrawals.
* Settled all daily transactions at close of business day.

EDUCATION

BURLINGTON COUNTY COLLEGE, Pemberton, NJ
Associate Applied Science -- Excepted: Dec. 1992
Concentration: Legal Technology
Legal Courses: Bankruptcy, Landlord Tenant, Civil Litigation,
Family Law, Legal Research, Real Property, Comparative Business
Entities, and Administration of Decedent Estate. Courses in
Accounting I & II, Business Law I & II, and Business Management.
Additional liberal arts and social science course.

ADDITIONAL INFORMATION

Language Skills: Fluent in Spanish
Computer Skills: IBM-PC (WordPerfect 6.0) wordprocessor
Canon VP 5000, Apple II.

DINAH WASHINGTON
8249 Sunnyvale Lane
Fort Myers, FL 32000
(813) 677-5552

EDUCATION:

Bachelor of Arts in Social Science, University of Puerto Rico,
1989

Languages: Fluent in English and Spanish, one year of French

Work Experience:

August 1991 to Present -- Marketing Coordinator, SPARTA SYSTEMS,
Inc., Gulf Breeze, FL.
Duties: Magazine advertising, copy writing, computer graphics
design, desktop publishing, accounts payable, inventory, data
entry, word processing, general bookkeeping, column building, and
some equipment assembly.

October 1988 to July 1989 -- Computer Operator, HOME ANALYST of
PUERTO RICO, Inc., San Juan, P.R.
Duties: Maintained computer input, output, and software
utilities, updated and organized clients' files, general
secretarial work.

Activities:

Psychology Students' Association

Special Skills:

Computers -- Knowledge of BASIC language, WordPerfect, Word Star,
Database Manager 2, dBase III+, Lotus, Harvard Graphics, SPSS,
Minitab, MicroTSP, DataDisk, Value Screen, GPS, and other
applications for IBM computers and compatibles.

Marketing Research -- Experience with research for the Ft. Myers
Symphony Orchestra and the First Presbyterian Church of Ft.
Myers. Work included development of research design, sample
evaluation, questionnaire testing and evaluation, interpretation
of results, computer analysis, and report writing.

Total Quality Management -- Assisted in TQM research study at the
Ft. Myers Naval Air Station. Work included questionnaire building
and personnel interviews on the effects of performance appraisals
on a TQM environment.

BILLIE CASTILLO
P.O. Box 2214
Tucson, AZ 86000
(602) 345-7121

SUMMARY: Offering 15 years of administrative and secretarial experience. Background includes payroll; administration of vendor payments; processing and verification of employees' expense accounts; resolution of personnel/benefits matters; procurement and distribution of office supplies, furniture and computer hardware/software; conference room arrangements; travel reservation arrangements; receptionist services. Resolution of outside customer inquiries. Responsible for confidential personnel files. Planned, organized, implemented any other administrative support functions of the Legal Department. Handled special projects as requested by the management. Possess superior organizational and managerial skills.

EXPERIENCE:

TUCSON VALLEY TELEPHONE COMPANY, Tucson, AZ

Administrative Assistant -- 1980 to Present

Responsible for payroll; administration of vendor payments; processing and verification of employees' expense accounts; procurement and distribution of office supplies, furniture, and computer hardware/ software. Handled and resolved personnel/ benefits matters. Administered various departmental award programs, i.e., Perfect Attendance, Safe Driving. Maintenance and filing of various departmental records, including confidential and proprietary records; conference room arrangements; travel reservation arrangements; receptionist services. Created the spreadsheet for the following: "original" spreadsheet for the Attorneys' Fees Report; Business Meals Report; Supply Inventory Report; Monthly Office Supplies Report. Developed an Office Supplies Order Form, to curtail unnecessary spending on office supplies. Possess various skills to operate PCs, including WordPerfect, Lotus 1-2-3, WordPerfect Office, Windows, etc.

Morrow: They all look like fine candidates.

Paradiso: Yes, I agree. And the winners are . . .

Ranking of Candidates for Receptionist/Secretary

<< 1 >>

CASTILLO, Bill	DOLAN, Sarah J
TETROCCI, Juli	ROBINSON, Jack
RANGEL, Myrtle	
RODRIGUEZ, Alb	
SANTIAGO, Dimi	

<< 0 >>

WASHINGTON, Di	CHENG, SuLee
MONNOLLY, Donn	PETERSON, Thoma
BULLOCK, Sharon	
RICIOSO, Jenny	

Morrow: Would you tell us why these candidates stacked up like this?

Paradiso: Billie Castillo and Sarah Jo Dolan both have all requirements, plus a desired skill. Billie Castillo has experience in several personal computer packages. Sarah Jo Dolan has telephone experience. Dinah Washington and Sharon Bullock meet only the minimum stated criteria. Remember, the candidates who win the listing race are those with the most "extra" skills above the bare-bones minimum requirements. But after that, humans take over. So your resume has to make sense to humans as well as to machines.

Morrow: Thanks, Jane, for leading us step-by-step through a new technology we'll all be dealing with soon.

BECOME WISE IN KEYWORDING YOUR RESUME

By now you understand Keywording 101, but are you ready to go for the advanced course?

The ultimate keywords come from each employer for each position. You can only make reasonable assumptions about what a specific employer will ask for.

Drawing on common recruiting requirements, the next section offers educated guesses about sample descriptors—keywords, buzzwords—for various occupations.

We first thought of drawing up huge laundry lists of keywords by occupation, regardless of where we obtained them. Upon reflection, we decided to present the lists *by source*, to give you a better picture of the perspective offered from different quarters. You'll be able to study three groupings:

1. Keywords from an executive recruiter.
2. Keywords from the database of an automated applicant tracking system (Resumix).
3. Keywords from print recruiting ads.

Examine all three to be sure you don't overlook clues to success in the new approach to presenting your best qualifications to employers.

Bear in mind that *these keywords are only examples.* They are offered as an educational tool to help you form the habit of labeling yourself.

After studying the lists below, **begin to keep a log of keywords as they apply to you in your specific occupation and industry**.

Jot down each keyword as you come across it, or as it occurs to you. When you're ready to do a scannable resume, you'll have a comprehensive checklist and will be less likely to miss an important word.

A SAMPLING OF KEYWORDS FROM AN EXECUTIVE RECRUITER

We asked a seasoned executive recruiter with a strong human resource background to start us off with basic examples of typical buzzwords for various occupations.

"Keep it simple," we suggested, and J. Herbert Wise obliged. Wise, a senior executive search consultant at Sandhurst Associates in Dallas, is a former vice president of human resources for major domestic and multinational corporations. Here is his starter keyword collection.

Accounting Manager

Supervisor	CPA
Manager	Accounts payable
BS Accounting	Accounts receivable

Brand Manager

MBA
Marketing
Advertising
Promotion
Consumer products

Chemist

PhD
BS Chemistry
Patent awarded
Research

Computer Manufacturing Manager

BS Ind. Eng. (Bachelor's degree in
    industrial engineering)
Surface Mount Technology
JIT (just-in-time ordering parts)
Quality Circles (management
    technique)
ISO 9000 (a program for quality
    standards)

Controller

CPA
Accounts payable
Accounts receivable
Payroll
Financial reporting

Human Resource Manager

Compensation
Benefits
Recruitment
Diversity
ADA
Training & development

Programmer

MS-DOS (Microsoft's Disk Operating
    System)
c++ (new programming language)
Optical Imaging (computer reading)
Windows 3.1 (Microsoft systems
    software)

Purchasing Manager

BS/BA
Vendor negotiations
Reduced cost
Improved quality

Salesperson

BS/BA
Exceeded quota
Will travel

A SAMPLING OF KEYWORDS FROM A
SOFTWARE DATABASE

Resumix, an applicant tracking system company headquartered in Santa Clara, California, is an industry leader in computer-driven technology that reads and sorts resumes. Resumix graciously allowed us access to its knowledge base. Several points about the sampling given here are important:

1. The Resumix keyword (knowledge) database is gigantic. Each category may have hundreds of keywords. This book presents only a handful of them from a sampling of categories.

2. Resumix does not assign the keywords to specific individual occupations, as we have done; the system searches in occupational

clusters. We think it's easier to follow a discussion of keywords in terms of specific occupations.

3. The choice of keywords for each occupation is a random one—it was made with the scientific methodology of throwing darts. In some cases, particularly in the technical occupations, we have no idea what the initials or abbreviations or processes mean. The words come straight out of the Resumix database and are reproduced as they appear there. (Resumix gets the keywords from customers and stores them as the customers direct.) If you're in one of the fields listed below and don't understand some of the terms we quote in these examples, maybe you'd better take the time to find out what they mean. They're hot with some employers.

4. We selected the keywords and assigned them to occupations. If errors exist—and we fervently hope they don't—they are solely the authors' mistakes. Blame us, not Resumix.

Accountant, Tax

IRS Amendments
TEFRA
TRA-86

Advertising/Communications Specialist

Applications Article Program
Articles
Booth Development
Collateral Material
Image Campaign
Promotional Materials
Sales Promotion
Special Advertising Supplement
Cable Television
Voice of America

Aerospace Engineer

Avionic Production Support
Gyro Design
Component Fatigue Test
Wind Tunnel Mdl Build
American Astronautical Society

Anesthesiologist

Fiberoptic Cart
Gas Calibration
Pain Management
Thoracotomy

Architect

Architectural Design
City Planning
Site Plan
Human Factors Engineering
Business Complex Building
Resort Design

Audio/Video Technical Specialist

Audio-Animatronic
Digital Recording
Interactive Video
Synchronization
Video Editing

Audiologist

Audio Evaluation
Audiolog Test Equipment
Audiometric Testing
Audiometry Certification

Bank Accountant

Annual Report
B&P Planning & Control

FIFO
Financial Modeling

Bank Financial Manager

Bankruptcies
CPU 999
Credit Guidelines
Skip Tracing
Uniform Commercial Code Filing

Banker

American Banking Association
Inter American Development
    Bank
RTC
Account Settlement
ATM
Bank Reconciliation
Commercial Loan Operations
Customer Conversion
Repossessions

Biology Laboratory Technologist

Aseptic Technique
Enzyme Handling
Immunoprecipitation
Parenteral Administration
Topical Administration
Genetics
Life Science

Carpenter

Cabinet Making
Carpentry

Chemist

Bioreactor
PK/PD Analysis
Wet Chemistry
Chiral Analysis
American Chemical Society
Gel Exclusion LC
Ion Exchange Resin C

Childhood Development Specialist

Child Development Center
Preschool

Educational Administration
Evaluation Training Programs

Civil Engineer

American Society of Civil Engineers
Civil Construction
Concrete Design
Correctional Facility
Preliminary Stress Analysis
Hydrology Trans Analysis

Clerical Specialist

Office Automation
Number of Words per Minute
Administrative Assistance
Appointments
Correspondence
Customer Relations
Dictation
General Office
Itineraries
Machine Transcription
Meeting Planning
Office Management
Personnel Assistant
Reports
Schedule Calendar
Secretarial
Shorthand
Spreadsheet
Staff Scheduling
Technical Typing
Travel Arrangements

Community Affairs Specialist

Community Development
Community Outreach
Community Project

Compensation Specialist

Anniversary Review
Equity Review
Incentive Plan
Job Classification
Merit Pay Program
Performance Evaluation
Salary Structure

Computer Specialist

Analog Computer
Compaq
HP 9000
IBM 3705
Mainframes
Optical Computer
Unix
Sun

Construction Manager

Building Permit
Construction Schedule
Gas Pipeline
Leveling & Grading
Gymnasium Building
Skyscraper Building

Consumer Protection Specialist

Consumer Assistance
Consumer Protection
Consumer Product Safety

Contract Administrator

Contract Negotiation
CPCM
Legal Issues
Proposal Preparation

Corporate Trainer

Clinical Internship
Compensation/Benefits
  Training
Cross-Culture Training
Employee Assistance
Sales Training
Technical Training
Total Quality Management
  Training

Customer Support Technician

2nd Tier Support
DOSS
Marketing Support
Product Support
System Level Problem

Dentist

American Dental Association
  Accredited
EFDA Certified
EFODA Certified
Local Anest Credential
OR Radiology Permit
Pit/Fissure Credential
Fixed Porcelain Restoration
Intra-Oral Bite Reg
Ultrasonic Scaler

Desktop Publisher

Aldus Pagemaker
Compugraphics
DCF
Harvard Graphics
PagePerfect

Dietitian

Amer Dietetic Assoc
Food Service Mgmt
Modify Menus
Portion Wrap
Diabetes Management

Drafter

Valid Logic
Autocad II
CADDS4X
CAD Tool Pathing
Test Pattern Genera

Economist

Economic Forecast
Industrial Policy
Minority Economic Impact

Electrical Engineer

IEEE
Lasers ElecOptics
Raychem Splice
Concept Design
Engineer Mgmt
PE License
R&D

Electronics Engineer

Aperture Synthesis
Radar Cross Sec
Optical Logical Dev
ESD Susceptibility
Ladderlogic
Engineer Standards
Interferometry
Charged Particle Beam

Employee Relations Manager

Career Counseling
Career Planning
Contract Negotiation
Downsizing
Grievance Adjustment
Redeployment
AHRSP
Soc HR Management

Employment Recruiter

AA/EEO Regulations
Applicant Screening
Applicant Tracking
Job Fair

Engineering Administrative Assistant

Concept Design
Detailed Design
Engineering Information Systems
Engineering Standards
Vendor Data Review

Environmental Engineer

Air Pollution Control
Emission Compliance
Groundwater Hydrology
Municipal Waste
Surf Water Hydrology
CA Assc Toxicology
Environmental Fate Protocol
Environmental Compliance

Equal Employment Opportunity (EEO) Specialist

Affirmative Action
Americans w/Disabilities Act

Female Owned
Project Hire

Field Service Technician

Documentation
Field Application Engineering
Field Engineering
Field Service
Installation

Foreign Policy Specialist

Canadian Affairs
NATO Policy
Refugee

Hazardous Waste Specialist

Biohazard Control
In Situ Vitrif
Nuclear Waste
Stabilization

Health Managed Care Specialist

Casework Services
Complaint Review
Eval Medical Service
Healthcare Administration
Medicare
Peer Review Process
Quality of Care

Histology Technician

Cryostat
Decalcification
Immunocytochemistry
Rotary Microtome
Tissue Fixation

Human Resource Specialist

401K
Defined Benefits
Disability Plan
Employee Benefits
Flexible Benefits
Health & Welfare
Pension
Service Award

Industrial Engineer

ASRS
Capacity Analysis
CAPP
DFM Tst Pt Guideline
Manual & Automation Standards
    Definition

Industrial Security Specialist

Background Investigation
Computer Security
Defense Industry Security
Industrial Espionage

Information Systems Specialist

Computer Simulation
Config Status Accounting
Data Modeling
Descriptive Flexfield
Video Conferencing

Instrumentation Engineer

ParaDyne
Programmable Controller
JET
Instrument Draft

Librarian

DIALOG
Online Library System
Wilson Journal Index
FFIC Classification
Materials Selection
Online Literature Search
Reference Desk
Subject Cataloging

Manufacturing Engineer

Automated Materials Handling
DNC
Real Time Process Control
SECS II
Vendor Data Review
Brazed Assembly
Fabrication
MRPS

Marketer

$2M-$5M Revenue
151–200% Quota
201+% Quota
3rd Party Relations
Account Penetration
Competitive Analysis
Competitive Comparison
Developed Launch Strategy

Mason

Brick Laying
Cement
Ceramic Tile
Tuck Point
Wallboard

Materials Engineer

Ceramic Engineering
American Ceramics Society
US Association Advanced Ceramics
Elastomerics

Mathematician

Society Industrial Applied Mathematics
Computer Modeling
Data Reduction
Mathematics Optimization
Queuing Theory

Mechanical Engineer

Fluid Dynamics
Shell Theory
Trajectory Generation
Internal Aerodynamics
American Association Mechanical
    Engineering
Actuator Servo Arch

Medical Office Specialist

CPR Processing
Doctors Orders
Medical Office
Medical Secretarial
Referral Coordinator
X-Ray Reports

Medical Records Specialist

Chart Deficiency
Health Plan Bill Standards
Medical Records
Professional Staff Bylaws
Release of Information Law
State Health Statistics Regulations

Mental Health Counselor

Cancer Counseling
Clinical Counseling
Crisis Intervention
Genetic Counseling
Group Counseling
Hospice Philosophy

Merchandiser

Analyze Fashion Service
Block Plans
Dollar Subsidy Analysis
Gross Margin Goals
In-House Private Label
Sales Maximization
Targeted Customers
Global Sourcing
Research Overseas Markets

Metallurgist

Process Metallurgy
Extrusions
Specialty Alloys
Tribology

Microbiologist

B'phage Lysate Assay
Infectivity Assay
American Academy Microbiology
Antimicrobial
DNA Blot
Restriction Enzyme
Direct Colony Count
Oligonucleo Design

Mining Engineer

Phosphate Mining
Aerial Mapping

Mine Safety
Powder River Basin

Network Protocol Specialist

Appletalk
Flashtalk
Novell Netware
Software Protocol
Yellow Page Service

Neurosurgeon

Craniotomy
Laminectomy
Neurosurgery
Ventriculoatrial

Nuclear Engineer

Design Review
Engineer Standards
BW Reactors
Power Ascens'n Test

Nurse (RN)

Catheter Care
Community Health Care Development
Infusion Therapy
Peripheral Line Management
Maternity/Child Rotation
Acute Care
Code 99
Disability Management
Intensive Care
Post-Op Care
Chronic Dialysis
Medication Administ
Suture Removal

Occupational Safety Inspector

Decontamination
Dosimetry
ESFAS
Radiation Protection

Optician

Contact Lens
Eyewear Fabrication

Optical Dispensing
Optical Retailing

Packaging Engineer

Analytical Ability
Organizational Skills
Materials

Painter

Airless Spray
Detailing
Matching Colors
Spray Equipment

Pharmaceutical Manufacturing Manager

Diagnostic Manufacturing
Novel Process
Biopharmaceutics
Cancer Diagnostics
Drug Formulary

Pharmacologist

2nd Messenger Fcn
Gastrointestinal
Mascarinic Rcpt Fcn
Vitro GI Mtlty Research

Plastics Engineer

Calendaring
Coinjection Molding
Cont Extrusion
Cont RP Laminating

Plumber

Drain Systems
Pipefitting
Septic
Waste Systems

Process Design Engineer

Dynamic Simulation
Feasibility Studies
Flare Systems
Flow Diagrams

Production Engineer

Concept Design
Engineer Management
PE License
Vendor Data Review

Public Health Service Manager

Aging Issues
Biomechanics Certification
Disease Prevention
Elder Care
Healthcare Policy

Pulmonologist

Arter Blood Gas Analysis
Bronchoscopy
Endotrach Intubation
Pulmonary Physiology

Purchasing Manager

Multitasking
Problem Solving
MMS
Asset Procurement
Contract Management
JIT

Radiologist

Autoradiography
Iodination
Radiobiological
S-35

Real Estate Agent

Asset Management
Commercial Leasing
Hotel Administration
Real Estate Appraisal
Realty
Residential Property
Surplus Property

Remediation Specialist

Bioremediation
In-Situ Bio-Remed
Site Assessment
Superfund

Reprographics Specialist

Blueprint
Change Control
Offset Press

Retail Marketer

Inventory Turns
Point of Sale
Sell-Through
UPC Scanner
Negotiate Commercial Terms
Educational Administration
Evaluation Training Programs
Work Study

Robotics Engineer

End Effector
ISO
Damage Toler Analysis
Matrix Method Analysis

Software Engineer

Commonsense Reason
Lisp
Xpeditor
Cross Debugger
Amiga
Microsoft C
Verdix Ada

Statistician

Biostatistics
Coeff of Variation
Standard Deviation
Stat Methodology
Stat Regression

Stock Broker

Brokers Call Rate
Dividend Reinvestment
Chicago Board of Exchange
NY Stock Exchange
Portfolio Mangement System
NASDAQ
Asset Valuation
Investor Relations
Surrender Value

Uniform Transfer Minors Act
12B-1 Plan
No-Load Fund
Price Earnings Ratio

Student Affairs Specialist

Academic Counseling
Career Development
Financial Aid
Need Analysis
Stafford Loans
Vocational Interest Test

Substance Abuse Counselor

12-Step Program
Clinical Supervision
Family Sys Theory
Prenatal Teaching

Surgeon

Laparotomy
Microsurgery
Organ Transplant
Surgical Asepsis
Tumor Transplant

Teacher

Adult Education
Adult Learning Theory
Computer Aided Testing
Drill & Practice Pr
GED
Instructional TV
Special Education

Theatrical Performer

Character Voices
Childrens Theatre
Comedy
Dance
Drama
Ensemble Work

TV/Movie Arts Specialist

Concept Design
Costuming
Creative Development

Feature Film
Industrial Film
Set Design
Animation
Foam Carving
Model Building

Word Processor

ABILITY
Displaywrite 5
Lotus Manuscript
Microsoft Word
Ready Set Go
Unix Editor

Vydec
WordPerfect 6.0
Wordperfect for Windows
Wordstar
XyWrite

Writer

Copy Editing
Creative Writing
Documentation
Installation Guides
Journalism
Manuals
Technical Writing

A SAMPLING OF KEYWORDS FROM ADS

To round out our presentation of words that capture a computer's attention, check this assortment we pulled from recruitment advertising pages.

Business Development Officer (banking)

Investment Management
Personal Trust Services
Commercial and Retail Banking
    Systems
Product and Service Enhancement
Investment Strategies
Estate Planning
Bank Trust Environment
Personal Finance Planning
Cultivate Relationships
Unwavering Commitment to Service
Regulatory Tax and Legal Procedures

Business Re-Engineering Consultant

Software Solutions
Concurrent Engineering
Effectively Applying
Senior-Level Engineering
Manufacturing Operations
Strategic Planning

Interpersonal Skills
Roi Investment Analysis Skills

Business Systems Analyst

Entrepreneurial
Proactive
Spirited
Project Management Tools
Alternative Tactical and Strategic
    Business Plans

Circulation Director (magazine)

Circulation Marketing
Budgets
Analysis
Distribution
Consumer Magazines
Three Years' Experience in Paid
    Circulation Management
Spreadsheets
Demographics
Databases

Direct Marketing
Bpa Audits
Bachelor's Degree

Contract Administrator

Intellectual Property Law
Software Licensing
General Federal Procurement
Gsa Schedules and 1412s
Excellent Verbal/Written
    Communications
Non-Standard Purchase Orders,
    RFP, RFQ

Corporate Communications Director

Advertising
Public Relations
Internal Corporate Communications
Marketing Management
Sales Merchandising
Creative Ability

Corporate Credit Manager (healthcare)

Collections Activities
Analytical Skills
Financial Analysis
Bankruptcy

Corporate Finance Director (airlines)

Financial Applications
Analysis Techniques
Financing Objectives
Financing Alternatives
BA in Business Adminstration
MBA

Corporate Investments Manager

Investment of Corporate and Pension
    Assets
Investment Accounting
Development of Investment Strategy
BA/MBA Finance, Economics or Related
    Fields
Excellent Communications Skills
Fixed Income Experience
Strategic Planning and Project
    Management Experience

Custody Administration Manager (banking)

Security Movement
Settlement Procedures
Custodial Accounts

Director of Security (banking)

Development and Maintenance of
    Systems
Procedures Designed to Protect Assets
Minimize Risk
Executive Protection
Investigative Operations
Experience Directing Security
    Function
Fraud
Forgery
Larceny
Burglary
Robbery
Employee Misconduct
Demonstrated Presentation
Writing and Verbal Skills

Employee Relations Specialist

BS/BA Business
4 Years' Human Resources Experience
Employment Law
Communication Skills
Interviews
Performance Appraisals
Organizational Development
Ethics
Leadership
Case Research Methods
Management Experience

Internal Auditor (industrial)

Operational Audits
Financial Audits
Certified Public Accountant

International Marketing Director (aerospace)

Commercial and Military International
    Sales
International Marketing

High Engineering Content Products
Engineering or Technical Degree

Management Consultant (information technology)

Experienced Systems Professional
Information Consulting Technology
Over-Achiever
Deep Technical Skills
Strong Business Acumen
Client Solutions
Open Systems
LAN and WAN (Local Area Network, Wide Area Network)
Re-Engineering Techniques
Large-Scale Systems Techniques
Relational Databases
Client-Server Technologies

Manufacturing Engineer

Flexible Packaging
Creative Manufacturing Engineer
Converting Industry
Printing Presses
Bag-Making Machinery
Extrusion

Media Manager

Corporate Media Budget
Media Sources
Market Strategies
Media Planning

Portfolio Manager

Tax-Free Money Markets
Tax-Free Bond Funds
Credit Analysis on Notes and Bonds
Client Presentations
Detailed Knowledge of Municipal Credits
Expertise in Derivatives
Computer Proficiency

Quality Assurance Director

Aerospace Manufacturing Environment
TQMS (Total Quality Management System)
Quality Improvement Standards
MBA
Exceptional Motivational Skills

Research Economist (insurance)

PhD in Economics
Research and Analytical Skills
Health Economics
Econometrics
Statistical Analysis

Senior Investment Officer

Quantitative Domestic Equity Management Firm
Equity Track Record
Global Equity
Domestic Fixed Income Experience

KEYWORDS DESCRIBING INDUSTRIES

Are you keyworded out after looking over the examples from an executive recruiter, an automated applicant tracking system, and recruitment ads? Hang on, there are just two more groups of keywords to go.

Now that you've got the knack of being alert to keywords for particular occupations, extend your range and notice keywords for industries. Here are a few examples drawn from the Resumix database:

Air Transportation

Airline
Airports
Landing Rights

Apparel/Footwear

Apparel Specifications
Athletic Apparel/Footwear
Menswear
Womenswear
Wrestling Apparel/Footwear

Automotive

Body Engineering
Body Layout Draft
Chassis Design
Quad-4
Biomechanics

Chemicals

American Institute of Chemical
  Engineers
Amer Chemical Society
Council Chemical Research
Corrosopmn Prevention/Control
Electrochemistry
Mechanical Separation
Pesticides

Freight Traffic

Article Classification
Carrier Negotiation
Chargeback
Customs Clearance

Motor Transportation

Class 4 License
DOT License
Land Vehicle Navigation
Valid Driver's License

Plastics

Antifogging Agents
Antioxidants
Biodegrad Additives
Flame Retardants
Halogen Compounds

Rail Transportation

Electrified Rail
Highspeed Rail
Rail Track

Textiles/Materials

Textile Development
Yarn Development
Fabric Production
Pattern Develop

KEYWORDS FOR INTERPERSONAL TRAITS

Most computer searches go after impersonal nouns like a duck chasing a June bug. These nouns answer the question of whether you *can* do the job.

Some employers, however, may ask the recruiter to search for nouns—or even verbs and nouns—that answer the question of whether you *will* do the job. These keywords describe the kind of person you are.

Courtesy of Resumix, here are some of the most frequently requested interpersonal trait keywords.

Ability to Delegate	Innovative
Ability to Implement	Leadership
Ability to Plan	Multitasking
Ability to Train	Open Communication
Accurate	Open Minded
Adaptable	Oral Communication
Aggressive Work	Organizational Skills
Analytical Ability	Persuasive
Assertive	Problem Solving
Communication Skills	Public Speaking
Competitive	Results Oriented
Conceptual Ability	Risk Taking
Creative	Safety Conscious
Customer Oriented	Self Accountable
Detail Minded	Self Managing
Empowering Others	Sensitive
Ethic	Setting Priorities
Flexible	Supportive
Follow Instructions	Takes Initiative
Follow Through	Team Building
Follow Up	Team Player
High Energy	Tenacious
Industrious	Willing to Travel

POLISHING YOUR KEYWORD SKILLS

How good are you going to be at using keywords? Well, how good are you at finding what you want in your telephone yellow pages directory, especially when the resource is not listed under the heading you think is appropriate?

Suppose you want to find a lawyer and the closest you can get alphabetically is "Lawn Mowers—Sharpening & Repairing"? Do you immediately look under "Attorneys"?

When you need to replace an electric toothbrush and can't find resources under "Electric Toothbrush," "Toothbrush" or "Tooth Fairy," do you then look under "Appliances—Small—Service & Repair" or "Drugstores" (which often are listed under "Pharmacies")?

Don't even try to look up all the discount stores within a day's drive because, in the yellow pages directory index, you're told to see "Heading Descriptive of Product or Service Desired."

The kinds of skills you need to trek through yellow pages directories are the same as those you need to write good keywords into your resume: *analyzing, classifying, synthesizing, comparing, identifying.*

How can you hone your keyword skills? Frank L. Greenagel, PhD, president of InterDigital, a career consulting firm in Lebanon, New Jersey, that markets the Looking for Work shareware, suggests the following two-part practical exercise:

1. Put an X in the blank by each category you think a company might search for if it was seeking a senior manager in public relations.

   _____ shirt-sleeves

   _____ bottom line

   _____ excellent communication skills

   _____ take charge

   _____ aggressive

   The answer: None of these terms is likely to be used. Employers are not going to search databases for terms like "shirt-sleeves" or any of the others that appear frequently in resumes, Dr. Greenagel says. "They will search for nouns—job titles, departments, companies and organizations, degrees, and so forth."

2. To prepare a computer-readable resume, Dr. Greenagel recommends this approach: Take a copy of your core resume and, using a highlighter, mark only the nouns you think a computer might use as keywords in a search. Then ask yourself whether those keywords adequately describe your work experience. "If not," he says, "you have some work to do."

Learning how to label yourself—how to keyword yourself—is well worth the necessary effort.

As your payoff for learning to keyword, you'll earn the best label of all: *Hired in the USA.*

4

The Right Look for Your New Resume

Chill the Frills and Add 15 Power Tips

OCR systems may have trouble interpreting exotic pages that feature bumps and grinds and lines and fancy type. Stick to conservative "vanilla" styles. As this chapter explains, when in doubt, don't flaunt your creativity. Use the power tips for scannable resumes instead.

At this stage of the resume revolution, there's little argument that, in scannable documents, less is more.

The best scannable resumes are elegantly simple: unadorned, uncluttered, and unpretentious.

Now that desktop publishing is widely available, a surprising number of people are sending out resumes that look as though they were prepared by someone who has just come into a fortune of computer fonts and hasn't gotten over it yet.

With their excess of typography, these documents are on a par with carwash flyers—busy with an infinity of thunderous bold headings and underlinings that blur together; a surfeit of check marks, bullets, and dashes; and little squiggly rules across the page.

Less is more for computer eyes too. This advice will hold good for the foreseeable future. Machines don't appreciate gargoyles or gingerbread—or even good writing.

As an example, take the lilting words created for the "Knute Rockne and His Fighting Irish" advertisement in the American Experience series, published by insurance behemoth Aetna:

> *For a man known as "Rock," Knute Rockne had an extraordinarily sweet smile. When he was pleased, his leather pumpkin of a face became a sea of wrinkles surrounding one of the great warm smiles of history. But he was indeed a rock . . . .*

Suppose, for the sake of example, the copywriter who penned these expressive words wanted to change jobs and thought it might be a good idea to include a mini-portfolio of work along with a resume.

Would it advance the copywriter's candidacy to include in the resume package those passages of gifted expression? Unfortunately, the process doesn't work that way. Until the copywriter is interviewed by a human recruiter, those beautiful words probably won't count for hiring points.

Even when seeking a top copywriter, a search engine in a computerized system can be counted on to bolt through a database and totally ignore a paragraph containing words like "rock . . . smile . . . pumpkin . . . wrinkles . . . history." Back into the electronic storage box the paragraph goes.

But as soon as the tracking system—patrolling for keywords that include competitors or major corporations—picks up the buzzword "Aetna," the copywriter rockets to the top of the list. Recruiters are impressed with copywriters good enough to have written for Aetna and Aetna's Madison Avenue advertising agency. If Aetna wanted that copywriter, they will say, we do too.

Employers assume that a copywriter with an Aetna label is able to turn out quality prose, and they look forward to reading it when the copywriter comes in for an interview.

Until that point, the classy writing doesn't help in the resume package.

Computers and their silicon pals don't care about the finer things in life. They cut to the chase. They get straight to the point. They eliminate the frills. If resumes were flavors and a computer could choose, the choice definitely would be vanilla.

In our talks with human resource professionals across the country, we found that systems dealing with resumes aren't equal in sophistication. Some OCR software makes sense out of boldface and many less common typefaces; others don't. The technology is constantly being improved as imaging industry competitors try to catch up or leap ahead.

We'll be more specific later in this chapter, but this is the concept to keep in mind: As a job seeker, you are flying blind in an increasingly automated job market. Most often, you won't know which technology is being used by what employer. You may not know how many times your resume will be photocopied or faxed, losing sharpness with each generation of reproduction.

During the next few years, your resume will be chasing a moving technology target.

The best advice we can give at this stage is to aim for a low- to mid-range common denominator in scanning and OCR technology. Executive recruiters and others who design their own systems are likely to have the low end of the technology; major corporations are likely to have the high end.

Because of the "flying blind" factor, we suggest that, for the next five years at least, the best resume is a vanilla resume.

HOW TO WRITE A VANILLA RESUME

The name of the game for OCR software is *distinctive edges to each character*. Each time a copy of your resume is made, it moves a generation away from the clarity of the original. The distinctive edges to each character become less distinct with each generation.

When the edges get mushy, or touch, or run together, your resume becomes hard to read. Hold the thought of distinctive edges in mind as you read these new rules for the physical production of your resume. Use these guidelines with almost every scanning system:

1. *To play it safe, stick to sans serif fonts. As a second choice, choose very popular serif fonts.* Sans serif is a typeface without serifs, the little strokes at an angle to the vertical lines of a character.

This is Times Roman. It is a serif typeface.

This is Helvetica. It is a sans serif typeface.

Serif characters can touch or run together. The capital letters E and F can look almost the same in a serif face, for instance. Although high-end systems can read almost all nondecorative typefaces when the original version of the text is presented, your resume will still lose clarity as a result of being faxed or photocopied to death. Even on originals, avoid decorative type-faces, such as the following examples:

USING TYPE THAT LOOKS LIKE THIS

WON'T GET YOU INTERVIEWS.

A SCANNER JUST CAN'T READ IT

no matter which you choose.

A resume to do its job

MUST BE QUITE CLEAN AND CLEAR.

While being artsy has its place,

IT REALLY ISN'T HERE!

Instead, print your resume in one of the nondecorative typefaces shown on page 76 or use one that is very similar.

The choices are drawn from a recent survey of America's most popular typefaces by Cynthia Hollandsworth, United States type marketing manager for Agfa Division of Miles, Inc.

The headlines are in 12-point boldface and the examples are in 10-point roman (regular). The selections in the left column are sans serif typefaces; those in the right column are serif typefaces.

To recap:

▶ When you're "flying blind," use a popular typeface.
▶ When you're fairly sure the *original* copy of your resume will be processed through an automated applicant tracking system, you can branch out and use popular, nondecorative typefaces, including those in the serif family.
▶ When you are certain the *original* copy of your resume will be rolling through *sophisticated* systems, you can chance using uncommon nondecorative typefaces.
▶ Never use a decorative typeface if there is a ghost of a chance it will take a spin through computer recruiting systems.

Ten Good Typefaces for Scannable Resumes

Helvetica
Want a Job?
Find a Job
In Ways You Never
Knew About Before...
The Technology is New
The Technology is Now!

Times
Want a Job?
Find a Job
In Ways You Never
Knew About Before...
The Technology is New
The Technology is Now!

Futura
Want a Job?
Find a Job
In Ways You Never
Knew About Before...
The Technology is New
The Technology is Now!

New Century Schoolbook
Want a Job?
Find a Job
In Ways You Never
Knew About Before...
The Technology is New
The Technology is Now!

Univers
Want a Job?
Find a Job
In Ways You Never
Knew About Before...
The Technology is New
The Technology is Now!

ITC Bookman
Want a Job?
Find a Job
In Ways You Never
Knew About Before...
The Technology is New
The Technology is Now!

Optima
Want a Job?
Find a Job
In Ways You Never
Knew About Before...
The Technology is New
The Technology is Now!

Palatino
Want a Job?
Find a Job
In Ways You Never
Knew About Before...
The Technology is New
The Technology is Now!

ITC Avante Garde Gothic
Want a Job?
Find a Job
In Ways You Never
Knew About Before...
The Technology is New
The Technology is Now!

Courier
Want a Job?
Find a Job
In Ways You Never
Knew About Before...
The Technology is New
The Technology is Now!

2. *Use a font size of 10 to 14 points.* Do not use anything smaller. To scanners and OCRs, small type is a tight fit. Type that's too big is like trying to absorb a wall mural in a single glance.

3. *Boldface is accepted by most systems.* Some scanners, however, do not handle boldface well. Unless an employer specifically tells you to avoid the use of boldface, go ahead and use it for headings. Capital letters can be substituted for boldface.

4. *Avoid italic text, script, and underlined passages.* Script and italics sometimes touch. Each of these three flourishes is trouble by itself; when two are paired (italics and underlining, or script and underlining), it's a recipe for mush.

5. *Avoid using graphics and shading.* When your resume is being scanned, the equipment is set to read "text," not "graphics." If the system is told to ignore graphics or shading, they are "zoned out." When systems get hung up attempting to read graphics or shading as characters, the result is pandemonium. Expect disturbance of your piece, too, if you make the mistake of using complex tables with leader dots (.......). Computers may trip over them.

6. *Use horizontal and vertical lines sparingly.* Some experts say flatly, "Use no vertical lines." If you do use lines, put at least a quarter-inch of white space around them. Computers will try to read lines. The horizontal lines may blur into characters, resulting in black globs that look like the inkblots on a Rorschach personality test. Vertical lines may be confused with the letter "l," also generating confusion in the computer's scan.

   Omit parentheses or brackets around any telephone area codes, as in (111) 222-3333. Most systems have no trouble reading the parentheses or brackets, but, as one authority says, "Why not improve your chances—leave them off."

7. *Avoid compressing space between letters.* Macintosh users in particular should beware of the temptation to pack everything onto one resume page. When you scrunch up your text, it becomes unreadable, even to wide-open computer eyes.

8. *Never use a nine-pin dot matrix printer.* A 24-pin letter-quality dot matrix printer is passable. A laser printer is best.

9. *Always send originals.* The sharper the resume—distinct edges, no dirty specks—the easier it is for a scanner to read, and the less you risk misinterpretation and error. You can't control the pathways your resume will travel, but you can start it out clean and crisp on its journey.

10. *Minimize the use of general abbreviations.* Many resume scanning systems are programmed to understand basic abbreviations like BA, MS, PhD, and other *standard, easily recognizable abbreviations.* Other systems will not recognize abbreviations unless they are told to do so by their search-engine dictionaries. When in doubt, spell it out.

11. *Maximize the use of industry jargon and abbreviations.* But use standard abbreviations, not weird, homegrown creations. You can logically assume that recruiters will instruct the search-engine dictionary to look for all the industry terms applicable to the job requisition. That is why it's important to use terms that buzz in your career field: "CAD" (computer-assisted design) or "COBRA" (Consolidated Omnibus Budget Reconciliation Act), for instance.

12. *Use a traditional resume structure.* Avoid complex layouts such as a page that simulates a catalog or newspaper page. Double columns don't go down well with some systems.

13. *Avoid a four-page resume on a folded 11" × 17" sheet.* Recruiters must tear these oversize sheets in half and scan page one, then flip it over to scan page two, and so on. This takes time, time is money, and your resume may be mistaken for waste paper and thrown out.

14. *Use light-colored, standard-size 8½" × 11" paper, printed on one side only.* You can use white, eggshell, or light beige or gray paper, but not hot pink, green, or any other vibrant color. Aim for high contrast between the ink and the paper.

    Relatively few computer resume reading systems come equipped with Hewlett-Packard software called HP AccuPage. One of its useful functions is to make text on colored paper easier to read. Don't count on strutting your paper resume before HP AccuPage or similar technology.

    Your surest bet is black ink on white paper.

15. *Only your name goes at the top of the resume, not a third party referrer.* When a third party (an executive recruiter or employment agency consultant) forwards your resume, the name of the third party should go at the end, not at the top of the document. A computer will try to read the third-party stamp as the name of the job seeker.

    Job fair sponsors, in particular, are guilty of creating this problem. In an attempt to be helpful, the sponsors slap a sticker at the top of the resumes of all the job seekers who attend. This practice helps corporate recruiters remember where the resumes came from, but it causes huge problems for the scanning systems.

As one corporate recruiter explains, "We scan in all the resumes we get at job fairs, but with that sticker it looks like the only person we talked with is named 'Career Expo.'" Stickers should be placed on the very bottom of resumes, or, even better from the machines' viewpoint, on the back.

16. *Your name should be the first text on a resume.* For the reasons just discussed, don't place other information above your name. As an example, you may cause grief to the system when you split your address and allow one line of it to appear above your name, like this:

	123 Main Street
JOE JONES	Memphis, TN 66688
	901 555-6666

The system may not even appreciate your name and contact information all on one line, like this:

JOE JONES   123 Main Street   Memphis, TN 66688   901 555-6666

Think of your name as a flag. Fly it over everything the system can scan.

16. *Explain your job title if it is strange or unfamiliar.* Do not change your job title for simplicity, but do explain it, in simple terms, in parentheses or a footnote.

17. *When faxing your resume, set the fax machine setting on "fine mode,"* *rather than on "standard mode."* It will take a little longer to send and cost a tiny bit more, but your resume will be far easier to read.

18. *Put no staples in your resume.* Even when removed, the previous compression may cause pages to stick together.

19. *Do not fold your resume.* If the crease falls across a line of type, it can be murder to read. Send your resume in a flat envelope, preferably with a light sheet of cardboard to keep it from becoming wrinkled or dog-eared. If you must fold your resume for some reason, be certain the fold does not occur along a line of text.

A CRASH COURSE ON REASONS FOR THE RULES

Most scanners and OCR software achieve high marks for accuracy on high-quality documents, but perform less spectacularly on resumes that have been passed around by photocopiers and fax machines.

The copy becomes "degraded." A resume once crisp and readable is changed for the worse and becomes difficult for applicant tracking systems to internalize accurately.

The mess created by degraded characters can affect your job search because faxing resumes has become a trend within the past two years. What once was a novelty is now commonplace.

Many employers who formerly requested a response by telephone or by writing to box numbers or addresses are now asking for replies by fax: "Fax us your resume," instructs recruitment ad after recruitment ad.

"General-purpose OCR software is not really suitable for reading faxed documents," says Stephen V. Rice, chief software engineer at the University of Nevada's Information Science Research Institute. "More and more people who do machine reading are using special fax recognition software," Rice explains.

Adding to the degrading of resumes is the fact that third-party recruitment services routinely photocopy them, often several times.

These figures, courtesy of Calera Recognition Systems Inc., show what happens to degraded characters. At least start your resume out as a high-quality document by choosing reliable fonts.

This is an example of a degraded letter "e" that does not look the way it should:

Joined characters are common if the scanner threshold is set too low, if the page is a dark photocopy, or if a serif font becomes indistinct and is set too close together.

Overlapping characters are common in italic text. The technology to improve printout of degraded characters is rushing ahead, led by Calera's Adaptive Recognition Technology, but you're still in the dark as to which systems will process your resume.

Split characters are common if the scanner threshold is set too high or if the page is a light photocopy. Serif faces aren't always readable: the sides are thick and the tops are thin. Splits make the characters look like unintelligible lines or curves. Sans serif type-faces, by contrast, tend to be evenly distributed all the way around.

A touching underline example is:

Signal

A degraded character image, at its worst looks like this:

From the disasters in the illustration, you can see why it pays to know the new rules of resume preparation.

AN IN-DEPTH UNDERSTANDING OF ABBREVIATIONS

To follow up on our suggestion that you avoid the use of *general* abbreviations, here are two examples prepared by Resumix linguist and computer scientist Mary Holstege. Both samplings are drawn from Dr. Holstege's collection of hundreds of variations actually used by data-entry operators at a wide variety of companies.

Your College Degree

In how may ways can searches be conducted for candidates whose backgrounds include a bachelor's (four-year) college degree? Among the hundreds counted by Dr. Holstege, here are 50 versions, quite enough to make the point that recruiters and clerks who enter the search requirements may enter the information in any number of ways.

The differences of opinion can be compared to how, in the absence of a formal filing system, office workers may not agree on where to file specific reports and papers. For instance, does the county tax bill go into the file for "accounts payable" or into the file for "taxes"?

Unless a particular system is preloaded to search for large numbers of synonyms—and not all systems are—your bachelor's degree and the employer's request for a bachelor's degree are twain that may never meet.

All systems can be instructed to search for synonyms, but, because it takes time to enter each synonym, systems that are not preloaded with a big bank of synonyms may, as a matter of underlying reality, have only a half-dozen or so for each word.

Look over this surprising variety:

A.B.
B.A.
B.Acc
B.Agr
B.B.A.
B.D.
B.E.
B.Eng
B.Engineering
B.F.A
B.L.A
B.Mus
B.P.S.
B.S.
B.S.W.
B.sc
B.tech
B.technology
B.Engineering
BA
baccalaureate
baccalaureate fine arts
baccalaureate of engineering
baccalaureate of fine arts
baccalaureate of science
baccalaureate of science landscape architecture
baccalaureate of science of landscape architecture
baccalaureate of sciences
baccalaureate of sciences landscape architecture
baccalaureate of sciences of landscape
architecture
baccalaureate business administration
bachelor
bachelor fine arts
bachelor of engineering
bachelor of fine arts
bachelor of law
bachelor of laws
bachelor of science
bachelor of science landscape architecture

bachelor of sciences of landscape architecture
bachelor business administration
bachelors
bachelors fine arts
bachelors of engineering
bachelors of fine arts
bachelors of science
bachelors of science landscape architecture
bachelors of science of landscape architecture
bachelors of sciences
bachelors of sciences landscape architecture

Your College Name

Besides "UCLA," in how many ways do keyboarders punch in keyword mentions for "University of California at Los Angeles"? Dr. Mary Holstege has found *450 variations!* We ran out of steam after keyboarding these 20 versions:

University of Ca. LA
University of Ca. in los angeles
University of Ca. at los angeles
University of Ca. at LA
University of Ca., los angeles
University of Ca., LA
University california of los angeles
University california of LA
University california los angeles
University calif of los angeles
University calif of LA
University calif los angeles
Univ of california of LA
Univ of california LA
Univ of calif. LA
Univ of calif at LA
Univ of Ca of LA
Univ of Ca at LA
Univ of Ca., los angeles
Univ Cal los angeles

When you mention your educational credentials, spell out the entire name or use a well-recognized abbreviation for the institution's name.

It's probably safe to assume that if your institution fields a sports team that gets frequent television coverage, the name used by sports commentators has been drummed into the national consciousness and is likely to be used in a search. These are some examples:

Pennsylvania State University: Penn State
Louisiana State University: LSU
Southern Methodist University: SMU
Texas Christian University: TCU
Florida Agricultural and Mechanical University: Florida A&M

EIGHT RESUMES THAT BAFFLE SCANNING SYSTEMS

On the following pages are eight resumes, chosen at random. Match them up with these comments on why scanning systems may be puzzled by them. **These examples are shown only to illustrate scanning problems, not content.**

Gloria L. Copeland
870 Camino Alga
Santa Clara, CA 92307
408 465-9678

Introduction: Over 20 years of progressively increasing responsibility with significant experience in microcomputers and office automation sales and marketing, direct fulfillment, office automation consulting and MIS project implementation.

Experience:
1985 - Pres. Computer Haven Superstores

1990 - Pres. **Director, National Order Center, Santa Clara, CA**
Managed a centralized inbound and outbound direct order fulfillment organization, including Telemarketing, Customer Service, and Operations. Managed a staff of up to 80. Grew business from average of $5.2 million per month to over $17 million per month in 10 months. Handled over 60,000 incoming calls per month.

1988 - 1990 **Director, Business Systems, San Clara, CA**
Responsible for the development, implementation, and support of operational systems in the order entry, shipping, and invoicing areas, Also responsible for strategic planning from MIS systems for the company. Managed the design and development of several new and enhanced systems, including an AS400 based order entry system, a branch office inventory control system, branch office automation projects, EDI systems, and an automated configuration systems. Managed a staff of up to 25.

1985 - 1988 **Senior Manager, Human Resources, Santa Clara, CA**
Responsible for the Management of the Corporate HQ Human Resources functions as well as all staffing and recruitment activities for the entire company. Managed a staff of 10.

1984 - 1985 ABC Corp. Saddle River, NJ
Manager, Recruitment and Staffing
Responsible for recruitment and staffing for Western Region.

1978 - 1984 APEX Group, Inc., Huntington, NY
Vice President
Managed operations of this executive recruitment and management consulting firm.

1974 - 1978 Jellico Corp., Office System Division, Houston, TX
Manager, Customer Relations Services
Responsible for managing team of field systems consultants, bid/proposal group, technical sales training group, and for training field Marketing Support Specialist. Managed a staff of up to 13.

1972 - 1974 American Telephone & Telegraph Corp., NY, NY
Staff Supervisor, Administrative Services Group
Responsible for managing office automation projects within the Long Lines Department of AT&T, as well as consulting on office automation projects within other parts of Bell System.

Education:

1972 - 1974   **Washington University, St. Louis, Missouri**
                   Over 60% of MBA course requirements completed.

1969   **Carnegie Mellon University, Pittsburgh, PA**
                   BS, Industrial Psychology

Military Experience:

1969 - 1972   **US Air Force**
                   Highest Grade: Captain

Miscellaneous:

Willing to Travel.
Willing to Relocate.

For many systems, this is a fine presentation. For systems that refuse to digest boldface, it's a problem.

PAUL W. LAW   9876 TIGER PLACE, WESTMONT, CA   (209) 688-9001

SENIOR OPERATIONS MANAGEMENT

Manufacturing, Engineering...Service/Product Support. Test/QA

Demonstrated success in facilitating rapid growth and generating substantial profit improvements in both turnaround and start-up environments. Skilled in directing all aspects of production and product support operations. Have introduced systems and procedures upgrades which improved productivity, enhanced product quality/competitiveness, and assured development/retention of major customers in multiple marketing channels. Progression of broad-based senior-level positions preceded by substantial background in systems and field engineering (at the national level) with Honeywell.

VICE PRESIDENT AND CHIEF OPERATING OFFICER - June 1991 to Present
ABC Computers Inc.

ABC is an integrator of IBM compatible computer systems, with market concentration in mass merchandising. In May of 1992, ABC filed for protection under Chapter 11 of the Federal Bankruptcy Law.

Recruited by the creditors committee, and hired by the President to attempt a turnaround of ABC. Reorganized operations to allow for immediate problem solving, inventory, production, and staff control.

Report directly to President. Operations area includes Customer Support, Systems Service, Inventory Control, Assembly, Production, Engineering, Quality, Warehousing, and Facilities.

- Introduced Quality Programs, Test Procedures, and Document Control Processes that cut customer calls by 50%.
- Devised and implemented a plan to turn stagnant inventory valued at $33 million into re-manufactured product that will generate over $13 million in revenue.
- Introduced staffing changes that allowed all levels of management to plan and solve problems.

DIRECTOR OF OPERATIONS - 1987 - 1992
The Smartshop Factory/Synergist Computers Inc.

SSF is an OEM designer and manufacturer of IBM compatible motherboards. SCI is a systems integrator (OEM, wholesale, government) spun off to expand product markets.

Recruited shortly after SSF start-up to solve critical operating problems. Upgraded and managed growth of Manufacturing, Test, and Service functions. In 1990, selected to also perform senior operations role at SCI.

Report directly to President. Directed Managers of QA, Purchasing, Production(2), Operations, and Customer Service (managed 18 supervisors). Managed combined budgets of $5.3 million. Full P&L responsibility for all aspects of Manufacturing and Technical Support.

- Introduced production and quality upgrades/controls instrumental in growth of annual Sales from zero to $50 million.
- Implemented Build-in-Quality Program for new products maintaining less than 1% reject rate.

EDUCATION

Undergraduate studies in Computer Technologies completed through New York College of Engineering in 1976; augmented by additional studies in Physics at Eastern Illinois University and ongoing corporate sponsored training in Quality, Human Resource Management, MBO, and Communications.

Paul Law's resume begins with his name and contact information on the same line, a practice not advised for good computer mental health. Moreover, it is set in small serif type, which is too condensed. If the text becomes degraded it will be illegible, as the above paragraph shows.

Ajax Technology

Technical Recruiting Specialists

887 S. Poway Avenue
Springfield, MA 76554
Telephone: 617-865-7744
Represented By: Darren Walkins

John M. Pool

SUMMARY:

Over 12 years of system software experience in Unix, MS-DOS, LAN, TCP/IP, GUI with X11, MS-Windows, and Windows-NT.

EDUCATION:

M.S. Computer Science, 1976, Rochester Institute of Technology, Rochester, NY
B.S. Chemical Engineering, 1974, Taipei University, Taipei, Taiwan

COMPUTER EXPERIENCE:

- Hardware: Sun SparcStation, IBM PC (XT thru 486), DEC VAX (750 thru 785), DEC PDP-11 (23 thru 70), Pyramid 90X, IBM (360, 370, 3031).
- Networks: X11 (R2 thru R5), RPC, NFS, TCP/IP, Novell, ISDN
- O.S.: SunOS (2.0 thru 4.1.3), Windows-NT, MS-Windows (3.0, 3.1), MS-DOS (3.1 thru 5.0), UNIX (V6 thru 4.3 BSD), SVR3, SVR4, VAX VMS (2.3 thru 3.5), RSX-11M, RT-11, OS/VS1.
- High-Level: C, C++, PL/I, PASCAL, BASIC, FORTRAN, COBOL, APL, ALGOL, SNOBOL, LISP
- Low-Level: Intel 8086, 8051, M68000, MACRO-11 (DEC), MACRO-32 (DEC), Zilog Z80

EXPERIENCE:

Principal Engineer
Multi-Systems Group, Inc.

1989 - Present
Springfield, MA

- Ported MS-Windows 3.1 programs to Window-NT as part of the in-depth technical report of the Windows-NT Software Development Kit (SDK). Designed and implemented object file analyzer in C++ for MS-Windows to allow programmers cut down program size.
- Led software group of six engineers developing local area networking software which provides PC-PC connectivity, PC to remote LAN access, and LAN-LAN routing using TCP/IP or Netware protocols. Programs were written in C with some 8086 Assembly using a SunOs development environment. Created both DOS character-based interface and MS-Windows based GUI. The software technologies involved in this project were: MS-DOS redirector, TSR, Netbios, SMB, TCP/1P, Novell SPX/1PX, and MS-Windows.

PUBLISHED PROJECTS:

- Contributed source code to the USENET community.
- Designed and implemented a biorhythm program for MS-Windows 3.1.
- Designed and implemented an Unix vi like screen editing system in VMS TECO composed of over 200 libraries, computer aided instructions.
- Designed and implemented a PERT analyzer.

John Pool's resume is presented by a third party, Ajax Technology. On extracted summaries, the name of the recruiting firm will often appear. The scanning system is likely to think Ajax Technology is the job seeker's name. The confusion can be straightened out if the position is hard to fill. But if the position is easy to fill, it may not be worth the employer's time to chase down the job seeker's name in the big electronic storage bin.

Dale B. Robinson

6457 Madison Street, Apt. #5
Pasadena, CA 93487
(415)432-8856, dale@mole.arc.nasa.gov

Summary Profile

Objective: Architect and lead for software projects, preferably in a supervisory role.

M.S. Computer Science (GPA 3.9/3.8) + M.S. Engineering (GPA 3.50/4.0), Washington State University, 1987. Over 5 years as software architect and technical lead, widely traveled in the northern hemisphere, multilingual.

Technical Strengths

- Distributed and Embedded Software, OOP, C++
- X/Open Portability guidelines for Open Systems
- Semaphores & shared memory, sockets, light-weight processes
- Sunview, X-window, OPENLOOK and MOTIF
- UNIX & VxWorks system calls and internals
- SUN, SCSI, VME, RS-232, terminal severs
- Database theory, SQL, Sybase

Supervisory/Team Strengths

- Ability to produce realistic software schedules
- Technical ability to train and troubleshoot
- Clarity and preciseness in task specification, grasp of the abstract, engineering and math knowledge
- Team spirit and approachability
- Confident and articulate
- System integration and test planning

Employment

Coarchitect/task supervisor, Acme Aeronautics, Software Division, since March 1991

Responsibilities: Provided technical leadership to groups of one to four member software teams. Responsible for planning and scheduling technical assignments and goals, defining and analyzing requirements, training, responding to customers, and contributing in performance reviews. Served in the capacities of Design and Code reviewer. Performed advanced system and network administration duties. Represented manager in liaison role in upper management meetings.

Technical Environment: Real time embedded system, Sun sparc, sparc 1-E, X/Open UNIX, VxWorks, HP-UX, X-Windows, vxWindows, C, C++, VME, SCSI, RS-232 and object oriented SW organization.

Projects: Real-time embedded software for airborne data acquisition system, using VxWorks (2-year project) +A complete simulation for the same on X/Open UNIX (1-year project).

Accomplishments:
- Principal Architect and Designer, library to hide the system dependencies between the target environment (VxWorks) and the simulator environment (X/Open UNIX) creating a virtual environment for applications.
- Coarchitect and Designer, framework library for the applications, controlling scheduling of tasks, memory and address-space management, concurrency control/synchronization, IPC, etc. Supervised other individuals.
- Defined the configuration management guide and set up the development and testing environment. Also defined software organization. Defined the organization of the distribution software as would be delivered to the customers. Coordinated the integration and delivery of the software.
- Developed a Rapid Prototype for the UNIX simulator with an assistant, commended for speed and quality.
- Designed and supervised the coding of a remote command shell (yacc/lex) for this system.

On Dale Robinson's resume, note the potentially lethal combination of underlining and italics. The third-party stamp is correctly placed at the end of the resume.

Graduate School Employment

Teaching Assistant, Math and CS Departments, Washington State University, 1985 - 1987
>   _Responsibilities:_ Instructed and assisted in instruction of Operating Systems, Databases, Fortran, Calculus,
>   Linear Programming, and College Algebra classes for undergraduate students
>   _Technical Environment:_ VAX, Unix, IBM 43XX, VM/CMS, Concurrent Languages Euclid and CSPK, Lisp,
>   Fortran

Research Assistant, EPA project on Water Filtration, PSU & UMC, 1984 - 1986
>   _Responsibilities:_ Designed and conducted experiments, analyzed data, wrote EPA reports and research
>   proposals
>   _Technical Environment:_ VAX/VMS, AppleIIe, Fortran

Overseas Employment

Software Engineer, Engineers Mexico Limited, Mexico City, Jan. 1983 - Nov. 1983

Commercial Product Experience

>   _Hardware:_ Sun 3/4, Sparc, VME, SCSI, RS-232, terminal servers, Mac, IBM PC, Vax-11, IBM 38XX and
>   43XX series
>   _Operating Systems:_ VxWorks, BSD and System V UNIX, SUN-OS, HP-UX, VMS, VM/CMS
>   _Languages:_ C (6 years), C++ (2 years), Modula-2, LISP, PL/I, Fortran, Pascal, 68020 Assembly, SQL

Graduate School

Thesis in Computer Science
>   "Automated generation of rpc code for Modula-2 modules" (MS Computer Science)

Class Projects:
- A mini NFS and RPC (UNIX/C)
- Simulation of a multitasking operating system environment (Concurrent Euclid)
- An SQL engine with query optimization (VM/CMS, PL/1, SQL)
- Software tools such as an editor, a pattern matcher, a source code control system (UNIX/C)

Relevant Graduate Coursework (credits)
>   Operating Systems (4), Database Design (4), Software Tools (3), Data Structures (4), Network Algorithms
>   (3), Computer Architecture (3), Artificial Intelligence (4).

Degrees
>   1986 M.S. Computer Science, Washington State University
>   1985 M.S. Environmental Engineering, Washington State University
>   1984 B.S. Civil and Structural Engineering, Computer Institute of Technology

Interests: Snow and Water Skiing, Windsurfing, Sailing, Hiking, Music, Tennis, Traveling

Submitted by
POWERS & POWERS INC.
P.O. Box 22222
Happy Valley, ND 77777
Ph: (600) 655-9876
Fax:(600) 655-9890

MARIANNE M. LUSK

29457 Holden Boulevard

Hollywood, CA 91657

805 - 656 - 1202

OBJECTIVE:
Position as Assistant Art Director/Set Designer for Film and Television

PROFESSIONAL ACCOMPLISHMENTS:

1989 to 1993
Harlow Productions, Pasadena, CA
Associate Show Set Designer

Set Design and Art Direction for theme park attractions involving conceptual design development; production and installation.

Areas of direct responsibility include: show set walls, scenic flats, platforms, murals, major props and artificial foliage. In addition, closely coordinated show action equipment, projection and audio equipment, special effects, rigging elements, theme and show lighting.

Principal Projects Include:
Fantasy World
Happy Quarters Review
School Pals Danceland
Heavenly Days

Additional Skills: AutoCAD, colorist, painting and illustration

1987 to 1989
Freelance Designer, Los Angeles, CA
Interior Design
Medium to large residential projects involving concept design, programming, space planning, material and finish specifications.

–1986 to 1987
Marquis & Associates, Laguna Beach, CA
Associate Interior Designer, Contract Design
Color and material specifications for Sizzler's National Remodel Program; original design for commercial food facilities; direct interfacing with clients.

EDUCATION:

UCLA Extension, Los Angeles, CA
1990 to Present
Certificate Program in Film, Television & Video

Woodman University, Hollywood, CA
1985-1988 Bachelor of Science, Cum Laude
Interior Design / Business Administration

Fashion Institute of Design and
Merchandising, Los Angeles, CA
1984 to 1986
Interior Design

PROFESSIONAL AFFILIATIONS:

Institute of Business Designers,
Hollywood, CA
Affiliate member, 1988 to Present
Participant in Continuing Education Units

American Society of Interior Designers,
Los Angeles, CA
1984 to 1988
Board Member, Student Chapter

REFERENCES AND PORTFOLIO
Available Upon Request

The effectiveness of the beautiful logo on Marianne Lusk's resume is wasted. Not only can't the computer read it, but it may give the system indigestion.

A second problem is the landscape (sideways) printing. Do not landscape your resume! Use portrait (vertical) printing.

A third problem for less advanced systems is the use of double columns.

JAMES B. HUMPHREY
1100 Balboa Park Drive
Kansas City, MO 88640
816-254-5576

James Humphrey's entire resume is written in italics. Script is also risky in scannable resumes.

OBJECTIVE

Long-term position in Applications Engineering, Applications Engineering management or Engineering support.

TECHNICAL SUMMARY

CAD Applications - VLSI Layout, CADAT Logic Simulation, DRC, SPICE, Electron Beam/Optical pattern generation, SYNTHAVISION solids modeling, Mechanical Design, DBMS
PC Applications - CROSSTALK, EXCEL, LOTUS, WORDPERFECT, FRAMEWORK, MIRROR, NORTON UTILITIES, Q & A, SMARTKEY, XTREE, TIMEWORKS (data management, spreadsheet and word processor)
Operating Systems - VAX/VMS, UNIX, VM370, CMS, MS-DOS, RSX-11, MAC
Compilers - BASIC, PS/I, FORTRAN, COBOL, C, IBM 370 Assembler
Interpreters - DCL, EXEC, Unix shell script, RSX Indirect command files

EXPERIENCE

Jan. 1977 to Feb. 1990:   *Acme Technologies (Formerly Welby)*
                            3100 Industry Way
                            Kansas City, MO 88605
                            Business: CAD/CAM

o   *Management of Western Regional Applications Engineers from 1977 to 1980; 11 direct reports.*

o   *Applications Engineer for VLSI and Mechanical Design fields. Pre/post sales support and marketing support. Customer training. Domestic and offshore experience. Applications programming.*

o   *Systems and applications problem solving a specialty.*

o   *Mechanical wireframe design and solids modeling.*

EDUCATION

1959-1963: Electrical Engineering; San Fernando City College and San Fernando State College.
1965-1970: Computer Science courses and Electronics Technology; College of San Ramon.
Corporate training in specific CAD/CAM Applications Packages and Operating Systems.

NOEL GOODMAN   **206-332-1599**
455 Yale Avenue   Seattle, WA 55402

EXPERIENCE

1984 - PRESENT	SENIOR PRODUCT MANAGER CONSOLIDATED SOFTWARE, INC. Management of software product development from inception to release. Responsible for coordination of design, scheduling, programming, packaging, documentation, marketing and product testing. Negotiated development contracts, determined development budgets and resource requirements, supervised other product managers. Strong emphasis on interactive design and editorial skills. Published several award-winning products, including Jam Session, Ancient Art of War at Sea and PlayMaker Baseball. Worked with floppy, CD-ROM and cartridge products. Accumulated expertise in consumer software, multimedia and video game industries.
1983 - 1984	SOFTWARE DESIGNER/PUBLISHER FREE SPIRIT SOFTWARE, INC. Developed and self-published "Competition Soccer" game, which received National Computing's Critics Award for Best Products of 1984. Responsible for design, packaging, distribution, marketing and sales.
1980 - 1983	CONSULTANT/LECTURER ZOO KIDS, INC. Taught classes and seminars on Zoo Kids programming and artificial intelligence to adults and children. Lectured at universities and computer fairs. Also chief editor of Zoo Kids newsletter.

SKILLS

HYPERCARD	Prototyped software designs in HyperCard on the Macintosh. Full knowledge of HyperCard development environment and tools.
WRITING	Wrote user manuals for published software products, including PlayMaker Baseball and Rock Session. Strong editorial skills.
MUSIC	Composed and arranged music for software titles and student movie projects. Full knowledge of MIDI, music sequencing and recording.

EDUCATION

1976 - 1982	SEATTLE STATE UNIVERSITY Bachelor of Arts equivalent in Interdisciplinary Social Sciences. Emphasis of study: computers and information sciences.

Two things are wrong with Noel Goodman's resume: the underlining, and the double dates on the education. A computer probably won't credit a bachelor's degree listed this way because it expects to see only one date. Indeed, the resume states "Bachelor of Arts equivalent." That dodge doesn't work on scanning systems. See the following section for a better way to handle a lack of a formal college credential.

Roberto Villareal
600 Calle Dario
Cincinnati, OH 44320
(513) 724-6453

SUMMARY: Sixteen years of computer development and data processing. The last seven years in TANDEM software development. My professionalism and use of structured methodologies result in high quality, user-friendly software systems.

EDUCATION: Cincinnati State University   BS Information Systems

JOB HISTORY:

FRIENDLY GROCERIES, Inc.   Cincinnati, Ohio

1988 - Present   Programming Manager

- Designed key components and performed extensive business analysis for the requirements definition of an SQL driven ORDER PROCESSING system. The cost savings in reduced inventory and superior service level was extrapolated to twelve million dollars.
- Directed system integration efforts, which included extensive testing and user reviews for a TANDEM SQL generated ORDER PROCESSING system.
- Implemented the pilot and subsequent roll out of the Order Processing System in conjunction with the warehouse distribution system in all of the Alpha Beta divisions.
- Engineered a DISASTER RECOVERY SYSTEM for contingency processing of store orders in case of a major disaster or the unavailability of a divisional processing center.
- Conceptualized and implemented innovative guidelines and procedures to standardize software across six divisions.
- Introduced new functionality and software products to assure that Alpha Beta has state-of-the-art RETAIL and DISTRIBUTION systems. This included writing COBOL SQL programs for inventory analysis, order cycle optimization and warehouse distribution processing.

WAYSIDE LIQUOR, Inc.   Cincinnati, Ohio

1985 - 1988   Programming Supervisor

- Developed and implemented a comprehensive financial system for company-wide processing of Accounts Receivable, Accounts Payable, General Ledger and Fixed Assets. Converted pre-existing (IBM based) financial systems to TANDEM.
- Coordinated installation aspects of a POINT OF SALE system for the retail chain. This included research and development for store specifications, installation, installation of software and documentation of system functions and procedures.

See the little hollow bullets on Roberto Villareal's resume? Computer eyes may see little "o"s and put a lot of Irish into it: "O Designed" . . . "O Directed" . . . and "O Implemented."
  Solid bullets and asterisks, however, are okay to use.
  Note how the horizontal lines work because there's space around them.

15 POWER TIPS FOR WINNERS

It isn't every day you write a resume. But every day of your life can depend on how well you do it.

In the new electronic age of marketing yourself, here are 15 power tips that can make the difference between a languishing job hunt and one in which you capture a job you love.

1. Number of Pages

"One page" is no longer the automatic answer to the question of how long a resume should be, even from resume readers for whom shorter has always been better.

The more keyword marketing points you present about yourself, the more likely you are to be plucked from an electronic resume database now, in six months, or a year from now.

After conferring with several human resource systems professionals, we are suggesting new benchmarks. It's not set in stone, or even in silicon. Feel free to deviate from it when you can justify your action, such as the fact that you spent your last college summer as a vice president of IBM and one page won't hack it. Or, if you want to trim your 45 years' experience back to the last 15 years, two pages will do nicely, thanks.

Unless the scanning system is swimming in electronic storage capacity, three pages, maybe four, per resume is about the maximum that will be archived. Try these benchmarks:

New graduates: One page.
Most people: One to two pages.
Senior executives: Two to three pages.

2. Cover Letters

For all jobs, include a cover letter with your resume.

Some recruiters of junior-level personnel say cover letters are not used for anything except slipsheets to separate a stack of paper resumes before they're fed into a scanning system. A cover letter takes as much electronic storage space as a resume. "Save a tree," is the environmental pragmatism.

Most recruiters, however, say they want cover letters to amplify the resume and that they are electronically stored along with the related resumes. Always include a cover letter when aiming for a top management job or in response to an ad.

Until you become a viable candidate for a specific position, chances are, says Resumix's Jim Lemke, your cover letter won't be reviewed. But once you make the short list, recruiters become hot to know every scrap of information about you.

Your cover letter should include a generous portion of keywords heralding your most impressive and relevant qualifications. If you are responding to a help-wanted ad, be sure to echo in your cover letter as many keywords from the ad as you legitimately can.

A cover letter also is a good place to tell the recruiter how you happened to send a resume. Here's what a top corporate recruiting executive, who wishes to remain anonymous, says on the topic of cover letters:

"In systems we considered, you can select a source for the resume. For example, it may have been generated by employee referral, customer referral, executive referral, newspaper advertising, job fair, and so forth.

"It is helpful to us if we know how you found out about the opening, or who referred you. If I place a $5,000 ad in the *Los Angeles Times*, I want to know how many resumes I got for my money. With our systems, I pull monthly reports that track where resumes are coming from.

"When I can't determine a source, I code it as 'U.S. Mail,' which to us means it is unsolicited. If I was reviewing a resume that started with 'Ben Hooks of the NAACP [National Association for the Advancement of Colored People] suggested that I send you my resume,' the statement would get my attention. If I coded it as 'NAACP' and was doing special recruiting, I might search that source code first," the recruiting executive says.

3. The 85 Percent to 90 Percent Rule

At Abra Cadabra, a well known software company headquartered in St. Petersburg, Florida, product manager Dan Harriger gives insights as to why you should stick to vanilla resumes, *especially when you're applying for a job many others can fill as well as you.*

"The password in computerized resume processing is percentages," he explains. "As an example, an employer who receives 4,000 resumes in a four- to six-month period prior to hiring seasonal employees needs to scan only 85 percent to 90 percent of them with a good degree of accuracy. Within those boundaries, the employer will find plenty of qualified candidates," Harriger says.

What about the 10 percent to 15 percent of resumes that come out looking like alphabet soup after scanning? "They lose. Resumes with garbled text are not corrected by hand because they're not needed. It is a waste of time and money when plenty of qualified candidates are being found by using the 85 percent to 90 percent rule," Harriger explains. His advice to job seekers: Think in terms of no-frills resumes.

4. Look for a Concept

Just as you color-coordinate your wardrobe, look for unifying themes for your resume. Choose a concept and then use the concept as a reminder to give specific examples of your skills in it. To illustrate, the function of marketing is a concept; trade shows, marketing research, and focus groups are the examples. Human resources is the concept level, and employee benefits, 401K plans, and compensation analysis are at the amplification level.

The keyword examples throughout the next chapter speak to this issue. Consciously focusing on a concept helps you stay on track without wasting space on nonproductive and irrelevant information.

5. Qualifying Problems

If age (too much of it) is your job problem, omit the years just as you would on a paper resume. Use only your last 10 to 15 years of work history. A computer won't care, and your resume will not be electrocuted because it doesn't have years. What happens when it reaches human eyes is another issue.

If you need to indicate that you are completing a college degree or other credential or that you have the equivalent of the appropriate credential, do not make the mistake mentioned earlier of putting down two dates alongside the name of an institution of higher education. To a scanning system, this is a dead giveaway that you're short of the requirements.

Instead, omit a date and place an asterisk next to the school name. *Be sure to place the asterisk a space away from the word, to prevent OCR error.* In a footnote, write what is true: "Pursuing," "Expected to complete in 1996" or "Bachelor's degree equivalent, as documented by accumulated course work, continuing education credits, and experience."

A computer will not penalize you for omitting a date, but will leave you in the wings when you use a double date next to a school name.

Should your problem be one of being a little shy of the requested years of experience, use only years instead of months and years.

Let's say the requirement is five years' experience and you have four. You began work in December of 1989 and it is now January

1994. If you show your experience as being "1989–1994," a computer will read it as five years. This treatment doesn't work when you're substantially short of the requested experience.

In case you're wondering, to fool a computer by writing down "five years' experience equivalent" doesn't work. The systems read numbers, not words, to determine years.

6. Updating Resumes

No matter how long it takes you to find a job, keep track of where your resume is lodging and update it regularly. Every six months is recommended, but, at a minimum, update it every year.

7. Multiple Resumes

Do not send multiple resumes, each showing you wearing a different occupational hat, to the same employer resume database.

Even in efficient manual systems, multiple submissions run the chance of comparison. But technology now gives them no place to hide.

Systems usually pull up everyone with the same name and telephone number. If you send one resume in as "M. N. Brown" and the other as "Marvin N. Brown," but show the identical telephone number, your multiple resumes will be spotted and the recruiter may have a negative reaction, "This person doesn't know what he wants to do."

Worse, if you are flagged as a falsifier, you risk being placed in a never-hire electronic lockup. You're blackballed. The summary for a potentially risky hire may be coded with some variation of "NH" (never hire) and remain in an electronic slammer long after the initial recruiter has left the company.

If you are determined to send in more than one resume within the same six-month period, use initials and a different telephone number, and switch your job listing lineup from the most recent job to the oldest job.

If you are updating, as suggested above, don't worry about the multiple resume problem: A tracking system automatically chooses the most recent resume by date received.

8. Professional Memberships Have Clout

If you've been debating whether you should lay out the money to join a professional society, here's one more reason why it's a good idea: The membership is golden on your resume.

As one human resource manager explains, "If a person is actively involved with professional societies and trade organizations—such as the Society of Women Engineers, Organization of Black Airline Pilots, and so forth—that should be on the resume. These are viewed as highly searchable 'skills' [keywords] a recruiter will hone in on when doing special recruiting.

"If I select just the skill of SWE [Society of Women Engineers], the search will give me all the resumes that mention that organization. Be sure to put the organization in your resume, as well as in your cover letter."

9. Following Up

After submitting your resume to a company you know uses an automated applicant tracking system, follow up within three or four days. Determine whether there are technical reasons why your resume didn't enter the system, and find out who is showing an interest in you.

Learn the name of the automated tracking system administrator or operator/verifier. Ask that person, "Did you receive my resume? Was I a match anywhere? Has my resume been routed? To whom? Which department?"

If you are stonewalled or asked why you want to know, simply tell the truth: "I need to follow up on my routing." Perhaps you have thought of additional and pertinent facts and want to send those data in a letter.

If you're an aggressive job hunter, call back at noon, or a little before opening hours or a little after closing hours, and ask to speak to the manager to whom your resume has been routed. Scripts on how to handle this follow-up marketing technique are offered in numerous job hunt guides.

The operative word in finding out whether you've "made the system" is *routed*. The jargon shows you have taken the time to know more about the hiring process than the average person. It hints you may be "one of us," making it easier to get what you want.

We should tell you that not all human resource pros agree with this advice. As one says, "With our system, I can enter a code for 'unsolicited phone call.' If a person has too many of those, he or she might get labeled as a pest."

Admittedly, it's a risk. The tactful, professional way in which you handle the call(s) will dictate whether a "pest" code is entered into the system after your name. If necessary, cultivate telephone relationships.

If you need a little help in strengthening a skill that daily becomes more essential—prospecting by telephone—read Joan Guiducci's *Power Calling* (Tonino, P.O. Box 2309, Mill Valley, CA 94942; (415) 383-4780; paperback).

In the very competitive job market of the 1990s, we recommend taking the risk and following up by telephone. As *Glamour* magazine columnist Marilyn Moats Kennedy says, call until you're told "Never call here again, you insect."

10. Testing the System

Suppose you call and you learn you have not yet "made the system." Call back in two weeks and ask again.

"Do you have an automated applicant tracking system? Am I in your database? I haven't heard from you and I thought these systems automatically sent acknowledgment letters. Can you check for me, please?"

Hold on while the operator/verifier or system administrator looks to see whether you're in or out.

If you're out, it tells you (1) the system can't decipher your resume, or (2) the staff is behind on its work. Ask which parts of your resume are garbled and volunteer to help clean them up. Make the offer even if you don't want the job. Use this as an opportunity to field-test your resume; learn what you should change so other systems don't go blind on the same points.

If you fail to get your document cleaned up, you won't be considered for a future job with the company that you do want.

If you're told that your resume is in the database but there's no match yet, take heart. It only means a match isn't on today's calendar. You've probably missed the current opening but perhaps a match will be made next week . . . or next year. The news is disappointing, but at least you're not hanging onto a false hope. You can forget this company for the moment and move on to the next opportunity.

(We don't want the above statement to mislead you into thinking you should look for one job at a time. Look everywhere, all at once. No matter what tools you are using, paper or electronics, it is a deadly mistake to pin your hopes on landing a particular job. Your job search should continue at full bore until the second week you are employed. Keep the momentum going just in case you discover during the first week that you really don't like the job well enough to stay put. Do you think one week is stretching things out? Some career advisers say to keep the momentum going until the second month you're employed!)

11. Using the Best First

Some systems stop reading after a specific number—say, 80—keywords per resume. That's why it's best to put your dates, company names, and job titles close to the start of your resume, instead of burying them at the end.

A search engine looks for "meat" in the body of a resume, and it may get a little addled when it doesn't see date, company, and job title grouped together. Computers, like people, expect to see certain things in anticipated places.

12. Using White Space

Every resume guide urges you to leave plenty of white space. "Type and white space should be arranged so that the reader's eye is drawn quickly from beginning to end." This good advice is equally true when the resume reader is a computer.

Computers like white space. They use it to recognize that one topic has ended and another has begun. A scanning industry maxim is "White space makes errors go away."

The use of white space is enhanced when your resume is as clean as newly fallen snow. If you're having your document photocopied, go to a top commercial copy shop that has advanced, expensive photocopy machines; the top-of-the-line machines turn out much better copies than your home machine, the library, or the local drugstore.

13. Using Common Language

Because not all systems have a full-fledged synonym table, try to maximize the "hits" between a position search and your resume by using words everyone knows. Don't describe a skill as "Can pound iron spikes." Instead, say, "Can hammer nails." Give your resume the "common touch" test.

14. Career Management

After you've been hired, continue to use applicant tracking systems as a career management tool. Try to learn as much as you can about how they work. Trade journals for human resource professionals often carry articles on the latest advances. Provide a yearly update of your resume to every database you hope will be a stepping stone on your career path.

15. Advancement on the Job

When you are hired, your resume moves from the applicant tracking system to an employee tracking system. It continues to work for you, day and night. You are always on tap for advancement opportunities when openings occur and management thumbs through the employee database. Job postings and internal promotions usually start with the employee tracking system.

Make friends with the system administrator and operator/verifier. You want to be sure your updates are entered promptly, and there's no better way than to be on good terms with the humans who get those machines moving.

5

Floor Plans for a Keyword Resume

Here's a New Format for Pleasing Computers and Humans Alike

A new kind of resume, the keyword resume, is suggested in this chapter. The keyword resume passes the scan test and appeals to human viewers. A description of the new approach is followed by a review of classic resume formats.

Millions of words have been written about choosing the right format for your resume. You'll find experts who swear by functional, chronological, hybrid, linear, power, performance, and accomplishment resumes. There's no shortage of format ideas from which to choose.

People who read resumes want the documents to be concise and clear and to reveal problem areas, thereby keeping the mediocre from their doors. *Straightforwardness is a virtue.*

People who write resumes want the documents to blow up their strengths and hide their flaws, thus thrusting them into good job interviews. *Artfulness is a necessity.*

Viewing a stack of papers a foot high, employers tend to wonder, "How fast can I tunnel through this mountain of resumes without getting a speeding ticket?"

Viewing a line of competitors a block long, job seekers tend to wonder, "How can I get every word of my resume read, after all the work I've put into it?"

You don't need field glasses to see that employers and job seekers don't sip one soda through two straws. What's quick and easy for employers is not necessarily healthy and good for job seekers. There exists, as management consultants say, a lack of goal congruence.

You must search for the format—how a resume is laid out and the data arranged—that will best bridge the gap between the employer's needs and your needs.

If you ignore artful formatting and your resume becomes an overstuffed bore, the employer's mind will be elsewhere.

Because your choice of format can strongly influence not only whether your resume is read but how it is perceived, we will review, later in this chapter, the principles of choosing the best format. First, here's our suggestion for an entirely new way of dealing with the issue in contemporary job search.

MEET THE KEYWORD RESUME

A keyword resume is one that places a summary of keywords near the beginning of the document. The remainder of the resume can be any format of your choice.

A Focus

The justification for a front-loaded keyword summary is simple. It's a matter of focus. Regardless of the varying technology used by vendors of automated applicant tracking systems, ultimately they all depend on finding particular words in your resume.

Recruiters cannot use nebulous terms and phrases to explain what they are looking for. They use keywords.

"A keyword resume forces people to put labels on their skills," says Lars Perkins, CEO of MicroTrac. "In our system there is no technical reason to begin a resume with keywords. But using bulleted key experiences and skills means you end up saying things in a more concise form."

"What we see happening," Perkins continues, "is that people embellish their experience with flowery language and they end up not really saying in a clear and factual way what it is they can do, have done, and wish to do. Starting with a keyword summary is a way of getting your priorities straight."

Resumix's Jim Lemke also thinks a keyword resume is a good idea. He agrees that putting your keywords in a paragraph disciplines your thinking and organizes your mind.

Lemke notes that "the longer a computer has to search for the facts it wants, the more chances it has to not see what you want it to see."

All automated applicant tracking systems that incorporate scanning technology have enormous or even unlimited keyword searching capability. Type in job titles like "loan closer" or "manufacturing supervisor" or "continuing medical education coordinator," and the name of anyone with that term anywhere in his or her resume will magically appear on the screen.

If, however, a recruiter wants to find a "continuing medical education coordinator" who attended Harvard College, the screen may show a continuing medical education coordinator who works with Harvard Graphics, or lives on Harvard Street, or whose last name is Harvard, or who works for Harvard Dry Cleaning, and so forth. This can happen in systems that are just catching up to the state of the art.

Resumix's patented artificial intelligence software is able to automatically place Harvard College into the education field, Harvard Graphics into the skills field, Harvard Street into the address field, and Harvard Dry Cleaning into the employer field. In addition to providing full keyword searches, this patented process automatically categorizes job seekers into as many as six occupational groups.

Is this enough? Some experts argue that if you can fit into more than six distinct career categories, you probably are a generalist who ultimately will be screened out in favor of applicants with superior depth in a target field. They endorse the old saying, "Jack of all trades, but master of none."

Further comment on the search-and-retrieval issue comes from Charles Borwick, vice president of client services for Restrac. Borwick says that almost any tracking system can distinguish Harvard University from Harvard Graphics and Harvard Street. The system simply looks for the words "Street," "Graphics," and "University." The issue arises when someone gives no other indicators except Harvard.

"That's when the truly sophisticated systems have to use a 'context marker' to understand which Harvard is meant," explains Borwick.

What's a context marker?

"Context markers are like section headings. For example, the heading 'Education' will aid the system in distinguishing which Harvard is meant. If the context markers are omitted, the system may misinterpret or not register the skill. Restrac makes use of context markers to improve its intelligence and reduce false 'hits,'" Borwick says.

Other fine systems, operating on a principle called "total recall with perfect precision," may be very attractive to job seekers. These include such excellent products as SmartSearch2, and most independent resume database systems. (For details, see our companion guidebook, *Electronic Job Search Revolution.*)

"Total recall" means occupational codes are not used. Everyone goes into one big electronic storage bin.

The "perfect precision" descriptive refers to the system's ability to call out from the total database any person who has a keyword related to the target occupation.

"Total recall with perfect precision holds advantages for career changers," says Peter Weddle, who operates Job Bank USA, an independent resume database in McLean, Virginia.

"From the individual's perspective, fixed categorization precludes that person from being identified in functional areas outside the assigned occupational categories, even if there is a high degree of skills transferability across functions," Weddle says.

Let's summarize the two divergent viewpoints. One holds that, in the real job market of the 1990s, you are unlikely to have enough expertise in more than a half-dozen categories to compete with candidates who specialize in any one of them.

The other viewpoint says it is better, particularly for career changers, to leave your options open. This school of thought contends that, if you're plucked from the wide-open database for an interview, you can gamble on dealing with your lack of specialization at that time.

The authors believe the first viewpoint is more likely to prevail today. We're living in what might be called "gold rush" times: The race for jobs belongs to prospectors who not only move fast and tenaciously but have the skills equipment to stake their claims. The 1990s is not a "gentleperson's job market."

By any measure, when you are writing a resume that will be read by electronic eyes, starting with a keyword summary is like paying basic bills before considering what to do with disposable income.

Once your keyword requirements are taken care of, you can kick back and figure out how best to use the remainder of your paper space to show why you're a top contender.

A Checklist

A second reason for beginning your scannable resume with a keyword summary is that many automated systems do not offer employers the option of viewing an original resume; they see only the extracted summary.

Think about that for a moment. Everyone appears on a standardized form with the same data in the same slots. It's like reading a racing form at the track and comparing the horses' statistics in each prior race. In regimented presentations, there's no way your specialness can speed you into the winner's circle.

Another roadblock is that some employers using systems that *have* the ability to store the original resume may elect not to use the full-text feature because it takes up too much electronic storage. Instead, they use only extracted summaries.

When a recruiter relies on only an extracted summary, the sentence structure and appearance of a resume don't count. The hiring decision maker will never see the resume.

The extracted summary shown in Figure 5–1 is a bare-bones fact sheet about an applicant. "Rap sheet" may be a more apt term. There are no frills, no niceties, no grace notes. Summaries are name-rank-and-serial-number versions of your experience, skills, and education.

Dual Purpose

A third reason favoring a keyword summary is related to differing technologies.

In some systems, the use of boldface is acceptable; in others, it can cause glitches. By offering your keywords in "roman" (regular, not boldface) type, you satisfy all the systems.

You still can use boldface, italics, underlining, graphics, or whatever else you want, to make the remainder of your resume attractive to human readers.

Imagine yourself as a recruiter wading through a hundred or more resumes without any visual relief in the use of typefaces: the sameness will cause your eyes to glaze over and soon you'll find yourself catching z's.

Conciseness

A fourth reason for our proposing that you write a keyword resume is that, even when humans (rather than machines) make the initial evaluation of your document, the keywords go straight to the heart of what resume screeners say they want: *truthful conciseness.*

During this time of the recruitment industry's transition from human screening to electronic screening, you can never be certain what or who will read your self-marketing piece.

The issue becomes more complex when you're applying to hundreds of potential employers. That's why we suggest simplifying

Received:
04/23/94
Source: CALtimes

JENNIFER T. ROBERTSON

Permanent
123 Good Way
Sunup, CA 92000

P (555) 328-3456

Category:

Sales

Education:

BA, Cal State Northridge, 85
Certified Sales Professional, 93

Work History:

90 to 94, Director of Sales, ABC Computer Networking
88 to 90, Sales Representative, Goodfellas Marketing Service
85 to 88, Management Trainee, Fly the Sky Airlines
83 to 85, Sales Trainee, Johnny Jumpup Shoe Company (part time)

Skills:

Spanish	Microcomputers	WordPerfect
Sign Language	Spreadsheet	Purchasing
Proposals	Phones	Invoice Processing
IBM PC	Customer Service	Presentations
Cold calls	Contracts	Seminars
Technology	Office Management	

Tracking:

Comments:

04/25/94   latuner   verified

Figure 5–1   Simplified Applicant (Extracted) Summary

your job hunting by adopting a keyword summary—the kind that pleases both technology and humans.

To recap, these are our four reasons for recommending the use of a keyword summary to begin your resume:

1. To give you the discipline of focus.
2. To make sure the right words are included when only the extracted summary is viewed.
3. To satisfy a computer's taste for plain vanilla presentations and a human's taste for creative graphics.

4. To appeal to the desire of human readers for truthful conciseness, apart from any viewing by a computer.

KEYWORD RESUMES: GOOD, YES; PERFECT, NO

Admittedly, if you don't match the profile the recruiters have been told to find, a keyword summary helps readers screen you out instantly.

In the job market days before the late 1980s, when employers did not have such an abundance of applicants, job seekers stood a better chance of talking their way into a hire, even when the match between the job's requirements and their own qualifications was weak. For those with strong verbal and persuasive skills, a good sales pitch often worked.

In these lean and mean times, don't count on that happening, especially when you're really wide of the mark. If your background bears little resemblance to the profile of skills and experience required for the essential functions of a position, you are going to be screened out at some point. It's just a matter of timing.

On the other hand, if your qualifications come within striking distance of the job order, you're in good shape. The recruiter may think, "This candidate's summary looks good. It's got the horsepower. I'll read the rest of the resume [or application or extracted summary] and see what else is under the hood."

Reading through a full-text resume, the screener sees what *you*, not computer programs, have written: you have a "hearty sense of humor," or you paid "80 percent of your college costs," or you have been complimented by former bosses as "being the best ever in the job."

Your keyword resume, after assuring the resume reader (machine or human) that the basic structure is there, invites exploration of the other parts of your package of skills and traits.

We've given you four reasons why you should construct a keyword resume when there is the slightest chance your resume will be eyed, digested, evaluated, and categorized by a computer before it is turned over to human intelligence.

But we don't want to leave you with the impression that a keyword summary is the only or, in all cases, necessarily the best format for a scannable resume.

Some critics will claim that the inclusion of a keyword summary at the beginning of a resume takes up valuable space and is redundant because most of the information is spelled out in the main body of the resume text.

For reasons already explained, this argument is weak when computers do the reading. When people do the reading, rushing through resume after resume as though they are doing an aerobic exercise, it's easy for them to forget what has been read. We don't think it's redundant to stress your key strengths; we think it's smart.

Job search is a reflection of life. With a few exceptions, there are no absolutes, no universals.

Every now and then, you find out that a friend landed a good job. When you see the friend's resume, it's terrible. You wonder why you bother spending time reading job search guides.

The answer is, we repeat, in job search there are no universals.

On this subject, do you know the story of a speaker at a sales seminar?

In explaining ways to counter sales resistance, he urged his audience not to let customers get away with universal phrases, such as "All insurance is a rip-off." Counter by asking, "All of them?" This will usually do the trick, the speaker concluded, "because universals are never true."

"Never?" came a reply from the audience.

We're sure you agree that what appeals to one employer may not appeal to another. Which accounts for resumes that fail to follow most rules of job search logic but whose owners find jobs.

That's why we're not hyping the keyword resume as the only answer under today's sun. We think it's a great answer, and resumes arriving from specialists who have worked on the hiring end of the automated tracking systems are beginning to include keyword summaries! They probably aren't consciously thinking of it as an "in" technique, but they're using it.

These human resource staffers have become familiar with the workings of the systems and have learned which resume techniques are effective in getting by the computers and landing the interviews.

As with any nascent technology, no one yet has enough experience with high-tech job search materials to make definitive, bet-the-farm statements about what universally works best and what doesn't work at all in scannable resume writing. We think the keyword summary will work for you but, because the technology is so new—and varied—we don't yet have adequate studies to back up our judgments.

In addition, the philosophical approaches by the vendors are a mixed bag.

Can you recall the dilemma that faced purchasers of VCRs in the late 1970s? Would the Beta or the VHS approach dominate the marketplace? VHS ultimately won out. Today's automated applicant tracking technology is in somewhat the same race for dominance. At this point, no clear victor has emerged.

After a few more years and millions of job transactions, we'll have a better basis on which to offer proven as well as reasoned advice.

In the meantime, we think the keyword resume is a logical approach to creating an effective job-finding tool for a job market in transition.

After a year of research, it is what the authors would use and will advise their families to use at this stage of the job search revolution.

So that you'll know what one looks like, here's our first example of a keyword resume. Gloria Green (a fictitious name, as are all the resume examples in this book) is based on a real person, a friend of one of the authors.

Sample Resume

Gloria Green

2204 Country Grove Lane
Kansas City, MO 66666

Work (816) 222-3333
Residence (816) 999-8888

KEYWORD   Marketing Executive. Sales Management. Product
SUMMARY   Management. Retail Industry. Information Systems.
           Competitive Analysis. $15-$30 million sales. National
Market Research. Product Introduction. Develop Launch Strategy.
Training Function. Product Marketing Department. Sales Support
Programs. Nationwide Travel. Supermarket Chain. Discount Stores.
Famous Name Systems. Well Known Electronics Inc. Industry Gold
Standard Retailer. Image Campaign. 151-200% Quota.
MBA Marketing-Duke U. BA-U of Mo.

Qualified by 16 years of progressive and increasingly responsible
positions in industrial and consumer marketing, sales and product
management.

KEY POINTS

- Established successful marketing and competitive
  analysis departments for the product lines responsible
  for 90% of revenues (over $100 million) of leading
  vendor.

- For international electronics maker, closed $5
  million order in 8 months (goal was 2 years).

- Planned and implemented most comprehensive product
  introduction in **Famous Names Systems'** history, from product
  launch to market dominance.

- Restructured employee training function for 100
  professionals.

- Documented systems requirements for top retailer,
  Industry **Gold Standard Retailer**, resulting in a contract
  with potential for $25-$30 million sales.

- Conceived "trade in" program for **Well Known Electronics Inc.**
  Increased overall sales by 500% in two years.

- Expanded overseas market in European Common Market nations
  by 60% in three years for present employer.

EXPERIENCE

FAMOUS NAME SYSTEMS   1984 to Present
Chicago, IL

Marketing Director

> Responsible for industry marketing and sales support
> programs; includes nationwide travel and industry contacts.
> Corporate authority on retail industry.

WELL KNOWN ELECTRONICS INC.   1981 - 1984
Whitewood, NJ

Product Manager to Major Account Sales Manager

> Secured $30 million of sales dollars in general
> merchandise and hospitality industry. Designed market
> acceptance test for successful product introduction.

INDUSTRY GOLD STANDARD RETAILER   1978 - 1981
Pittsburgh, PA

Director, Administrative Operations

> Responsibilities for billion-dollar retailer included
> operation of 60 discount general merchandise stores.

EDUCATION

National University, Master of Business Administration   1983
University of Missouri, Bachelor Arts in English   1978

PERSONAL STYLE

My work is a high priority. I use strong organizational and
motivational skills to get it done in a timely manner without
budget overruns. Others say I'm savvy, analytical, quick to size
up a situation, and have a winning sense of humor.

QUESTIONS AND ANSWERS ABOUT KEYWORD RESUMES

Q. What is the best way to write a keyword summary?

A. Follow the concept of the "inverted pyramid" used by journalists. That is, put the most important parts first, and work your way down to the least important parts.

The pyramid style of writing can be compared to a nursery tale:

"Once upon a time . . . ," and then you wait until later in the story to find out what it is all about.

With the inverted pyramid style of writing, you let the reader know immediately what it is you're trying to say:

Snow White is qualified to direct people of short stature, by her more than 15 years' experience in household management at the managerial level and a degree in apple buying from Smart University.

In your keyword summary, get to the more important stuff immediately. The usual order is to list the job title, occupation, or career field you want. Next come your most important sales points, especially the essential skills for a specific position. End with your education information.

As a new graduate with little experience, you may or may not want to alter the lineup, reversing education and experience. Your choice depends on which assets are your most salable.

With so many college students holding jobs today, you may be able to avoid presenting yourself as a raw beginner. By careful packaging of your paid and unpaid work (three months here, four months there, and so forth), strive to come up with the experience level everyone wants: three years or so. *Never sell your potential when you can sell your qualifying experience.*

When you have substantial work experience, lead with your skills rather than your education. When you have a knock-out education from a well-known institution and scant experience, open with education. The decision has to be made on a case-by-case basis.

For everyone, from untried teen to seasoned executive, the key is to use logic. Begin with the position, occupation, or field in which you are job hunting, and follow up concisely with your most qualifying keywords.

Q. Are you required to repeat each keyword in the body of your resume, merely to give it credibility?

A. No; it may even be better to use a synonym that reinforces what you are claiming. If an OCR errs on one word, it is unlikely that it will err on the synonym. You are increasing your chances of getting a "hit." *Synonyms protect you against OCR errors.*

To illustrate, suppose in your keyword summary you use the initials "MBA." In the body of your resume, spell out "Master of Business Administration."

If you use the term "database" in your keyword summary, identify the name of the database in the body.

If your keyword summary contains the term "news anchor," use "tv journalist" in the body of your resume.

If "RN" is in your summary, write "Registered Nurse" in the body.

No matter how you construct your keyword resume, you must make it easy for a human reader to see the direct relationship of its components. Your resume must hang together, with meticulous internal logic. Its body must provide a match with your keyword summary.

If your summary causes the computer to bring you to the screen and a recruiter can't find the exact keywords repeated in the main body of your resume, the recruiter may be curious and want to solve the puzzle. A little mystery can work to your advantage. The recruiter may pick up the telephone and call you for clarification. Now you have still another chance, on the telephone, to stand out from the crowd and sell yourself.

Q. Can you stuff your keyword summary with the necessary terms, but merely make a general statement covering those words in the body of your resume?

A. Yes. An example is given in the next section, in the resume for Roy Apple Kunz. The keyword summary identifies a number of accounting software programs by name, but the main body simply states that he is learning new accounting programs. Knowing he has his keyword bases covered, Kunz uses his remaining space to communicate other strengths.

Which is it better to do, use the body of your resume for synonyms, or introduce new information? We can't give you an off-the-rack answer. Each resume should be customized, depending on your qualifications and the demands of the occupational job market in which you're working.

As a generalization, we would use remaining space in the body of the resume to communicate additional strengths, when doing so does not undermine your keyword strengths.

Q. Does it matter to a computer how long or how wide the keyword summary block is?

A. Your summary can be as long as it needs to be, but use judgment. Save as much space as possible to show what kind of a person you are, reflect your personality, indicate judgment, and toss in extra appeal—"I'm quick at learning new information" . . . "I enjoy challenges."

   You can use the remainder of your space to suggest positive work traits. We've never heard of anyone not getting a job because of positive work traits. But you need the opportunity to indicate that you offer these kinds of benefits:

- Dependability.
- Sense of humor.
- Cheerfulness.
- Leadership.
- Persistence.
- Calmness during crisis.
- Sense of responsibility.
- Promptness, with no cheating on time.
- Good memory.
- Mature judgment.
- Desire to do good job; always trying.
- Ability to accept criticism and learn from it.
- Skill in time management.
- Ambition.
- Care with employer's property.
- High energy.
- Willingness to do extra work.
- Good powers of observation.
- Ease in meeting people.
- Ability to elicit confidence.
- Enthusiasm.
- Resourcefulness.
- Success in relationships.
- Analytical approach.
- Resilience.
- Care in meeting deadlines.
- No lingering hostility from being outplaced.
- No lingering hostility from anything.

Q. What about margins?

A. Technically, most scanning software is not confined to a minimum margin on the left and right sides of the paper. A computer doesn't care. Aesthetically, about a half-inch on each side is the bare minimum; one inch is better.

   We can envision a resume in which the keyword summary pushes the limits to a half-inch on each side, but the body of the resume expands the margins to one inch.

Q. Should I separate my keywords with commas, periods, semicolons, bullets—or what?

A. It's your choice. We use periods because it's simple. Remember that a few scanners have trouble reading boldface—including bold bullets—but most handle it with ease.

Q. Is the keyword summary somewhat like an accomplishment or qualifications summary?

A. Yes, in the sense that all opening summaries on resumes are "hooks" to encourage further reading.

   We can compare keyword summaries with hardwood floors, while accomplishment or qualifications summaries are more like carpeting.

PRACTICE MAKING KEYWORD SUMMARIES

Do a quick reading of the resume of Roy Apple Kunz (pages 118–119). How many keywords can you find that may be usable in a keyword summary?

We found 35 keywords in Kunz's resume. *The choice of keywords is subjective. You may or may not agree with our findings.*

Resumix's Jim Lemke, who read Kunz's resume, makes a good point. Lemke says 35 keywords may be too many for human eyes, that 25 keywords is a safer ballpark number when people are reading for conciseness.

On the other hand, it can be argued that the more keywords you use, the luckier you get.

The word-count in keyword summaries can be viewed as a tradeoff between computers and humans. Here's another instance of "Time will tell."

Roy Apple Kunz
1111 Shadowridge Drive, Apt. 300
Horizon, California 92000
(415) 696-6966

Objective: Controller of small company; Assistant controller
of medium-size company.

Experience:

1989-present   **Controller.** Best Bet Lighting Co., 7200 Camino
Vida Roble, Carlsbad, CA 92009. Immediate
superior: Carol Ann Hodges, president.

- Handled accounts receivable, collected 98% of
  outstanding accounts.
- Oversaw payroll contractor; changed vendors to
  save company money.
- Provided all financial reports. Never a problem.

1987-88   **Controller.** Remarkable Concrete Inc., Suite #A,
1600 Holly Avenue, Escondido, CA 92025. Immediate
superior: Jack Dodge, president.

- Managed tight cash flow situation by
  implementing aggressive collections policy
  and negotiating payment schedules with vendors.
- Upgraded associate's position by delegating
  receivables as well as payables data batching
  responsibilities.
- Used Timberline software for data control.

1986-87   Short-term temporary assignments while attending
computer and accounting classes (including Lotus
1-2-3).

- Prepared closing schedules for Mooncor Inc.,
  year-end audit; prepared mid-year statement for
  same.
- Reconstructed accounts for McGraw-Hill as
  extended temporary assignment.

1985-86   **Controller.** CoCo Contracting Inc., Suite #412,
4040 East Horace Road, Phoenix, AZ 85000.
Immediate superior: Peter R. Bagel, president.
Firm was a minority business enterprise initially
associated with the Tallow Companies, Contracting
Division.

- Formulated chart of accounts for new firm and
  prepared year-end statements for CPA.

- Suggested operational cost cuts to accommodate period of stalled business activity due to project shut-down.
- Worked with Tallow personnel to improve cooperation on several vital projects.
- Established format and procedures for project cost systems; educated field personnel on cost reporting.

1982-85   **Controller.** Boot Contracting Company Inc., 1400 South 11th Avenue, Phoenix, AZ 85000. Immediate superior: Cecil C. Boot, president.

- Joined the firm when cash flow problem was severe. Formulated and implemented plan to ease situation by refinancing debt and renegotiating contract in process.
- Developed leasing requirements and policies. Executed cost cuts.
- Assisted company president in reactivating construction line of business by providing financial analysis and coordinating needed bonding. Maintained all project data.
- Represented company in outside audit. Prepared all corporate tax filings.

1978-82   **Controller.** Mooncor Inc., 1434 West 12th Place, Sun City, AZ 85000. Immediate superior: William R. Kunz (father), president.

- Joined company at start-up and developed accounting systems and procedures for retail solar business.
- Expanded base accounting to include sales commissions and state sales tax.
- Produced multi-state inventory costing schedule to detail variances in pricing of solar parts.
- Represented company's position in yearly formal audits; prepared all payroll related filings, W-2 annuals and sales tax forms.

Education: **Master of Arts**, Anthropology, Washington State U. **Bachelor of Arts,** English, Cal State, Northridge

Ongoing program of accounting courses.

Practical coursework with Lotus 1-2-3; general knowledge of computer functions. Learning additional accounting software programs.

Taken directly from Roy Apple Kunz's resume, here are the 35 terms we thought the summary could include:

1. Controller.
2. Assistant Controller.
3. Accounting Systems.
4. Accounts Receivable.
5. Accounts Payable.
6. Payroll.
7. Financial Reports.
8. Cash Flow.
9. Aggressive Collections.
10. Payment Schedules.
11. Timberline.
12. Lotus 1-2-3.
13. Closing Schedules.
14. Mid-Year Statement.
15. Reconstructed Accounts.
16. Year-End Statement.
17. Cost Systems.
18. Cost Reporting.
19. Refinancing Debt.
20. Cost Cuts.
21. Financial Analysis.
22. Outside Audit.
23. Corporate Tax Filings.
24. Retail.
25. State Sales Tax.
26. Multi-State Inventory Costing Schedule.
27. Audits.
28. Payroll Related Filings.
29. W-2 Annuals.
30. Sales Tax Forms.
31. MA.
32. Washington State U.
33. BA.
34. California State U.
35. Computer Functions.

Although Kunz's resume could embrace some or all of the above words, is it necessary to use each in a keyword summary? No, it isn't.

Pick and choose the terms most likely to cause a computer to make you a screen star.

From the first cut, these are the 25 keywords we selected for Kunz's summary:

1. Controller.
2. Assistant Controller.
3. Accounting Systems.
4. Accounts Receivable.
5. Accounts Payable.
6. Payroll.
7. Financial Reports.
8. Aggressive Collections.
9. Payment Schedules.
10. Lotus 1-2-3.
11. Closing Schedules.
12. Year-End Statement.
13. Cost Systems.
14. Cost Reporting.
15. Refinancing Debt.
16. Financial Analysis.
17. Corporate Tax Filings.
18. Multi-State Inventory Costing Schedule.

19. Audits.
20. Payroll Related Filings.
21. W-2 Annuals.
22. Sales Tax Forms.

23. MA.
24. BA.
25. Computer Functions.

In Chapter 3, we recommended that you begin accumulating a log of keywords as they apply to your occupation and industry. Let's assume Roy Apple Kunz did exactly that and accumulated a log of 275 keywords. We sort through and find the intriguing terms listed in Figure 5–2 (page 122).

These are great keywords but Kunz can't lay claim to all of them. The check marks in the YES column show those Kunz can legitimately claim.

Now Kunz's 34-keyword summary contains these items:

1. Controller.
2. Assistant Controller.
3. Accounting Systems.
4. Accounts Receivable.
5. Accounts Payable.
6. Payroll.
7. Financial Reports.
8. Aggressive Collections.
9. Payment Schedules.
10. Lotus 1-2-3.
11. DacEasy Instant Accounting.
12. One-Write Plus Accounting.
13. Quattro Pro.
14. Microsoft Excel for Windows.
15. Closing Schedules.
16. Year-End Statement.
17. Cost Systems.
18. Cost Reporting.
19. Refinancing Debt.
20. Financial Analysis.
21. Corporate Tax Filings.
22. Multi-State Inventory Costing Schedule.
23. Audits.
24. Payroll Related Filings.
25. W-2 Annuals.
26. Sales Tax Forms.
27. MA.
28. BA.
29. Computer Functions.
30. Budget Systems.
31. Cost Accounting System.
32. General Ledger System.
33. Estimated Tax.
34. Tax Laws.

Kunz's keyword log really came in handy as a memory nudge. Nine keywords from the log were bellringers and Kunz could honestly claim them. When they are added to the first cut's 25, the final total is 34 keywords.

	YES	NO
Budget Systems	✓	
Cost Accounting Systems	✓	
Fixed Asset Systems		✓
Forecast Systems		✓
General Ledger Systems	✓	
Hogan Systems		✓
Liability Systems		✓
American Institute of CPAs		✓
California Society of CPAs		✓
Estimated Tax	✓	
Tax Laws	✓	
DacEasy Instant Accounting	✓	
One-Write Plus Accounting	✓	
Quattro Pro	✓	
Microsoft Excel for Windows	✓	

Figure 5–2 Selections from Roy Apple Kunz's Keyword Log

We made other changes in Kunz's resume, such as removing addresses and people to whom he reported (these can be supplied if requested) and trivial material. We added several items he had forgotten, which came to mind when compiling the keyword summary. In addition, for human eyes, we added a "Personal" section designed to project him as a living, breathing human being, rather than as a clone or a cipher (a problem with the original resume).

For computer eyes, we used roman (regular) typeface on the keyword summary, and followed it with a splash of boldface for human eyes. Notice how we broke up the keyword summary into four paragraphs for easier reading.

To summarize keyword resumes, we repeat: We do not insist there are only two ways to format a resume: our way and the wrong way. All of us are still taking reasoned guesses in high-tech job search and welcome any feedback you'd like to share.

At this stage of automation in the hiring industry, we think that beginning with a keyword summary and following with the format style that best fits you is what will work best.

ROY APPLE KUNZ
1111 Shadowridge Drive, Apt. 300
Horizon, California 92000
(415) 696-6966

Controller. Assistant Controller. Accounting Systems. Accounts Receivable. Accounts Payable. Payroll. Financial Reports.

Aggressive Collections. Payment Schedules. Lotus 1-2-3. DacEasy Instant Accounting. One-Write Plus Accounting. Quattro Pro. Microsoft Excel for Windows.

Closing Schedules. Year-End Statement. Cost Systems. Cost Reporting. Refinancing Debt. Financial Analysis. Corporate Tax Filings. Multi-State Inventory Costing Schedule. Audits.

Payroll Related Filings. W-2 Annuals. Sales Tax Forms. Computer Functions. Budget Systems. Cost Accounting System. General Ledger System. Estimated Tax. Tax Laws. MA. BA.

1989-present   **Controller.** Best Bet Lighting Co., Carlsbad, CA

- Handled accounts receivable, collected 98% of outstanding accounts.
- Oversaw payroll contractor; changed vendors to save company money.
- Provided all financial reports. Never a problem.

1987-88   **Controller.** Remarkable Concrete Inc., Escondido, CA

- Managed tight cash flow situation by implementing aggressive collections policy and negotiating payment schedules with vendors.
- Revised general ledger system; estimated tax.

1986-87   Short-term temporary assignments while attending computer and accounting classes.

- Prepared closing schedules for Mooncor Inc., year-end audit; prepared mid-year statement.
- Reconstructed accounts for McGraw-Hill as extended temporary assignment.

1985-86   **Controller.** CoCo Contracting Inc., Phoenix, AZ

- Formulated chart of accounts for new firm,
  advised owner on tax laws and prepared year-end
  statements for CPA.
- Suggested operational cost cuts; established
  cost systems; educated field personnel on cost
  reporting.

1982-85   **Controller.** Boot Contracting Company Inc.,
                       Phoenix, AZ

- Joined the firm when cash flow problem was
  severe. Formulated and implemented plan to
  ease situation by refinancing debt and
  renegotiating contract in process.
- Developed leasing requirements and policies.
  Executed cost cuts.
- Assisted company president in reactivating
  construction line of business by providing
  financial analysis and coordinating needed
  bonding. Maintained all project data.
- Represented company in outside audit.
  Prepared all corporate tax filings.

1978-82   **Controller.** Mooncor Inc., Sun City, AZ

- Expanded base accounting to include sales
  commissions and state sales tax.
- Produced multi-state inventory costing schedule
  to detail variances in pricing of solar parts.
- Represented company's position in yearly formal
  audits; prepared all payroll related filings,
  W-2 annuals and sales tax forms.

Education: **Master of Arts**, Anthropology, Washington State U.
                       Bachelor of Arts, English, California State U.

                       Practical coursework with Lotus 1-2-3, plus
                       several other accounting courses.

Personal: Good with puzzles, enjoy bridge, chess and
                       problem solving. Prefer small, friendly office.
                       Previous employers have rated me "among
                       best hires ever."

A REFRESHER COURSE IN RESUME STYLES

The personal marketing pieces designed to get job interviews have only three basic categories:

1. Chronological.
2. Functional.
3. A combination, or hybrid, of the first two.

But there are many variations on the Big Three formats.

To refresh your memory in case you haven't recently prepared a resume, this section gives capsule descriptions of the most popular formats, including their strengths and weaknesses.

If you need more help, a number of authoritative authors have penned fine books on resume writing and you may want to consult several of these.

Chronological Format

The information on your employers is organized in reverse order of occurrence. You begin with your most recent experiences and work backward, showing dates alongside each employer.

Pros

1. Most employers say they prefer this format because it's simple and direct.
2. The format showcases a steady work record that reflects constant growth.
3. The reader can zero in on a consistent upward track record.
4. The format works well in conservative industries—banking and health, for instance.

Cons

1. The format guarantees rejection for those who have gaps or setbacks in their work history.
2. This is not the format of choice for new graduates because they rarely have substantial work experience. Listing a job or two is like decorating a concert hall with nothing but a couple of chairs. It looks empty.

3. The format does not help the employer to visualize the future—what a person *can* do. Because it is a testament to the past, it sometimes is called the "obituary" format. If you died, it could be quickly adapted to a death announcement.

4. Highlighting accomplishments and skills without cluttering the resume takes a practiced hand.

Functional Format

In this format, the information is organized by functions or skills—marketing, organizational prowess, human relations, or program development, for instance. Ideally, these are the functions and skills of the job being sought.

The grouping in a functional format is done without regard to time sequence or where each competency was gained. Dates and employers are capsuled at the very end of the resume. Until a few years ago, employment specifics often were omitted entirely. The strategy still works in some cases, but omitting employment names and dates is risky.

By selectively focusing on your qualifications for the kind of job you want, the functional style downplays irrelevant jobs, spotty work records, and career reversals.

Pros

1. This format works well for career changers because it's ideal for presenting transferable skills—those skills that can move from one occupation to another. You can omit experiences that do not apply to the kind of work you want. If your dream job requires good budgeting skills, you can emphasize the experiences that show you can handle budgets, ignoring the nonrelated fact that you once had a job in which you learned to string guitars.

    This format is good for military personnel who are getting out of uniform and into the civilian job market.

2. For young job seekers, using this format maximizes scant work experience.

3. The format is useful when earlier job titles did not do justice to your real contributions and accomplishments.

4. The format can be helpful when the best work you did was not in recent jobs but earlier in your career.

5. When your most impressive assets have come from volunteer work, set up your resume in this format.

6. You may have gaps in your work record, big black holes that are difficult to explain. In today's market, enlightened employers do not consider being out of work for two years a big deal; others do. If you have an on-again, off-again work record, you'll want to consider this format.

7. Your presentation will not be boring. Well done, it reads with interest from word one.

Cons

1. Many employers find this format suspicious. No matter how sizzling the self-marketing piece, their question is: "What is this person trying to hide?"

   Usually, the problem, from the recruiter's viewpoint, is job hopping, an older applicant trying to disguise age, a lack of career progress, underemployment, an employment gap, an educational shortcoming, or too little relevant experience.

   The format itself can be a cause of instant rejection: It is not forthright.

2. Unless it's handled deftly, the format can be as confusing as an "I Love Lucy" episode in a chocolate factory.

Hybrid Format

A combination format takes the best from the chronological and functional styles. It combines the self-marketing of the functional approach with the credibility of the chronological version.

Pros

1. For those with enviable career records, the hybrid—or one of its offspring—is the format of choice. Many employers say the past is the best indicator of the future. The hybrid format sells what you can do and shows your history to prove it.

2. The hybrid or combo approach is especially good for those closer to the end than the beginning of their careers. It shows you are not stuck in a rut with old-fashioned resume skills, and you can limit the chronological portion of your resume to the last 10 years' experience. Even if your accomplishments and skills extend back much longer, keep your resume to a length of two pages and you won't have room to spell out all 30 years of your experience.

Cons

1. Mishandled, the hybrid format can be a mishmash.

Linear Format

The linear format, a favorite of outplacement agencies, is a chrono-logical format with lots of selling and lots of white space. Each accomplishment is presented on a line-by-line (linear) basis.

The spacing rivets attention on achievements and makes the resume easier on the eyes. The linear approach usually skips a job objective and a personal data section, but it opens with a qualifications summary.

(Without a job objective, the resume does not say what you are looking for, but you can supply this missing information in a cover letter. Otherwise, you're really saying, "I'm good. Here's what I've done to prove it. Can you use me?")

Pros

1. The choreography of the information is very appealing in a linear presentation. Like good advertising, it captures attention.
2. The lack of a job objective can work in your favor if you want a comparable or better job than the one you have left or are leaving. On the theory that a manager can manage anything, your record speaks for itself.

Cons

1. Because there is no job objective, the format can leave the reader unclear about the level and type of position you seek. If you're willing to consider a lateral or downscale position, this format doesn't work very well.

Power Format

The power format is virtually the same as the linear format. It opens with a qualifications summary and uses abundant white space.

Other do's for the power format: Omit objectives, age, marital status, and graduation dates—unless you know these will work to your advantage. Speak of specific accomplishments, not duties or responsibilities. Tailor your resume to each job.

The pros and cons are similar to linear resumes.

Performance Format

Another version of the hybrid format, a performance resume begins with a powerful opening statement, sometimes termed the "20-second resume." The opening statement summarizes your overall professional capabilities. Three or four major professional accomplishments follow, and the section ends with a short statement of your working style and the kind of person you are.

The body of the resume lists several more accomplishments, your experience, and your education.

In the performance resume, you can include pertinent affiliations, but should definitely leave out salary or requirements, hobbies or sports (unless relevant), marital status, number of children, references, or the statement "References available."

Pros

1. This format betters your odds with speed readers because it immediately shines a light on your assets.
2. Your originality is on display.
3. You can easily adapt the resume to each job you are going after.

Cons

1. You need some writing skills to attempt this format. It will look clumsy if not put together in a sophisticated manner.

Accomplishment Format

This version of a hybrid resume features a list of *impressive* career achievements. It tilts toward the functional format, but a chronological work history follows the list or is woven into it.

It opens with a job objective in a career field, such as Manufacturing Engineering. Next comes a bulleted qualifications statement of five or so main points: years of experience in the field, track record, specific skills related to the job objective, areas of specialized knowledge, or product expertise.

A healthy list of six or more eye-catching accomplishments comes next, followed by a bare-bones statement of experience (company name, job title, and number of years there—but no dates) and education.

Pros

1. This format is helpful to people who have been laid off from responsible positions, have not worked in their field recently, or have been out of work for more than a few months.

Cons

1. Because this format is closely identified with functional formats, it is subject to the same problems.

GET THE KEYWORD HABIT

From now on, the art of being wise is the art of knowing what *not* to overlook—at least where your resume is concerned.

Back in the century before Christ was born, the Roman poet Virgil observed *Non omnia possumus omnes*—We are not all capable of everything.

As the 21st century approaches, it becomes ever more urgent for us to be able to identify everything we are capable of.

We can do that by mastering the concept of keywords and using them on our resumes.

MERGING KEYWORD SUMMARIES WITH VARIOUS FORMATS

With the exception of the performance resume, keyword summaries look good atop the other formats described here. Compare the following pairs of resumes and note the impact of the keyword sections.

KAREN J. WHITE

1102 Central Lane   Message (816) 565-6622
Kansas City, MO 66666   Home (816) 565-2121

Objective: An opportunity to demonstrate my administrative, decision-making and managerial skills in the health care field with a Fortune 500 company or leading medical research facility.

EXPERIENCE:

1989 -- Present **Corporate Health Care Administrator**

In charge of corporate health care program for **Acme Manufacturing Corp.**, Kansas City, MO

1985 -- 1988 **Director, Corporate Benefits**

Developed and directed the **Rock Island Railway Corporation's** employee benefits program. Was hired as assistant director and promoted to head of department after one year.

1980 -- 1985 **Hospital Administrator**

Oversaw operations of **Western Hospital's** 100-bed hospital in rural Kansas, along with one skilled nursing facility for 80 elderly residents.

-- Developed pre-construction marketing program for skilled nursing facility.

-- Directed startup of skilled nursing facility, hired management staff and developed to full operation.

1975 -- 1980 **Program Director, Membership Services**

Directed member recruitment/retention program and professional education program for the **Kansas Association of Retirement Homes.** This statewide organization represents not-for-profit retirement facilities, which provide housing, health care, and community services for the elderly. Increased retention rate by 50%.

1972 -- 1975 **Director, Physical Therapy**

Directed physical therapy program for **St. Joseph's Hospital** in Centerville, MO. Developed and managed inpatient and outpatient department, working closely with neurosurgeon in developing exercise programs for post-op patients.

1968 -- 1972 **Physical Therapist**

Staff Physical Therapist at **Tripler U.S. Army Hospital**, Honolulu, Hawaii. As a staff therapist, had responsibilities for working closely with neurology department in developing exercise programs for post-op patients.

EDUCATION

MBA, University of Missouri, 1974 -- cum laude
BS in Physical Therapy, University of Iowa, 1967

PROFESSIONAL AFFILIATIONS

Society for Human Resource Management
National Association of Employers on Health Care Action
American Health Care Association

KAREN J. WHITE

1102 Central Lane   Message   816 565-6622
Kansas City, MO 66666   Home   816 565-2121

Health Care Administrator. Director. Assistant
Director. Physical Therapist. Physical Therapy.
Hospital Administrator. Program Director. Director.
MBA. BS. U.S. Army. Benefits Package. Company Health.
Contractual Packages. Corporate Health Care Management.

EXPERIENCE

1989 -- Present Corporate Health Care Administrator

In charge of corporate health care program for
Acme Manufacturing Corp., Kansas City, MO. Develop
specifications for company health benefits package;
negotiate all contractual packages with provider(s),
as well as direct a staff of five. A member of the
corporate executive committee.

1985 -- 1988 Director, Corporate Benefits

Developed and directed the **Rock Island Railway
Corporation's** employee benefits program. Was hired as
assistant director and promoted to head of department
after one year.

1980 -- 1985 Hospital Administrator

Oversaw operations of **Western Hospital's** 100-bed
hospital in rural Kansas, along with one skilled
nursing facility for 80 elderly residents.

-- Developed pre-construction marketing program
for skilled nursing facility.

-- Directed startup of skilled nursing facility,
hired management staff and developed to full
operation.

1975 -- 1980:   Program Director, Membership Services

    Directed member recruitment/retention program and
professional education program for the **Kansas
Association of Retirement Homes.** This statewide
organization represents not-for-profit retirement
facilities, which provide housing, health care, and
community services for the elderly. Increased retention
rate by 50 percent.

1972 -- 1975:   Director, Physical Therapy

    Directed physical therapy program for **St. Joseph's
Hospital** in Centerville, MO. Developed and managed
inpatient and outpatient department, working closely
with neurosurgeon in developing exercise programs for
post-op patients.

1968 -- 1972: Physical Therapist

    Staff Physical Therapist at **Tripler U.S. Army
Hospital**, Honolulu, Hawaii. As a staff therapist, had
responsibilities for working closely with neurology
department in developing exercise programs for post-op
patients.

EDUCATION

Masters Business Administration,
        University of Missouri, 1974
        -- graduated cum laude
Bachelor of Science, Physical Therapy,
        University of Iowa, 1967

PROFESSIONAL AFFILIATIONS

Society for Human Resource Management
National Association of Employers on Health Care Action
American Health Care Association

SHARON MEYER

321 Spring St.
Center City, NJ 99999
(609) 754-0029

Objective/Summary

An administrative/managerial marketing position with a national corporation...More than 15 years experience as a sales and marketing professional ... Demonstrated strong organizational skills, combined with a high level of creative energy ... Easily handle multiple projects at the same time with equal competency ... Am viewed by clients as a knowledgeable, reliable, and resourceful manager with a positive attitude.

Sales and Marketing

-- **Built diversified client base** with consistent sales volume from $500,000 to $1 million over a two-year period.

-- **Systematized a highly effective quick response program** for clients and customers that produced twice the repeat business. Increased sales by 51%.

-- **Managed all phases of projects for customers** on local, national and international levels with competent, reliable and personalized service. "Best client pleaser on staff," according to company president.

-- **Developed sales** of $1.5 million annually by working closely with design professionals to meet specific customer product specifications.

-- **Designed and delivered presentations** to major architectural and design firms to develop strong business relationships.

-- **Developed and implemented marketing plan** generating 400% increased sales leads, 45% more new sales and 25% increased company profits.

-- **Launched new sales program** with client architect, interior design and engineering firms.

-- **Performed public relations** representative functions for company to professional organizations, such as chamber of commerce and advertising and marketing associations.

-- **Planned and managed 14 corporate events and 16 trade shows** for company.

-- **Aided development of 13 company advertising campaigns.**

Management Skills

-- **Trained dealer sales representatives** on company products.

-- **Designed, coordinated and executed** more than 200 seminars on various company functions and products.

-- **Developed three-state sales territory.**

Education

-- **Master of Business Administration**, Marketing, University of Pennsylvania

-- **Bachelor of Arts**, Interior Design, Ohio State University

SHARON MEYER
321 Spring St.
Center City, NJ 99999
609 754-0029

Keywords   Sales Professional. Professional Selling
            Skills. Marketing Professional.
            Marketing Plan. Organizational Skills.
            Creative. $1.5 million sales. 51%
            Increased Sales. Sales Leads. Clients.
            Customers. Architectural Industry.
            Interior Design Industry. Corporate
            Events. Trade Shows. Trainer. 200
            Seminars. Advertising Campaigns. MBA.
            University of Pennsylvania. BA. Ohio
            State University.

Sales and Marketing

    --   BUILT A DIVERSIFIED CLIENT BASE of repeat and
          new business resulting in consistent sales
          volume from $500,000 to $1 million over a
          two-year period.

    --   SYSTEMATIZED A HIGHLY EFFECTIVE QUICK
          RESPONSE PROGRAM for clients and customers
          that produced twice the repeat business.
          Increased sales by 51%

    --   MANAGED ALL CUSTOMER SERVICE PHASES OF
          BUILDING PROJECTS for clients on local,
          national and international levels, resulting
          in a reputation for delivering competent,
          reliable and personalized service. "Best
          client pleaser on staff," according to
          company president.

(The rest of this resume remains the same)

Johnathan Jennings-Krepp
42116 Highway to the Stars
Seattle, WA 98000
(206) 233-4453

Objective:

Social worker position providing counseling to children and their families.

Highlights of Qualifications

-- More than 5 years' experience working with children and their families.

-- Enthusiastically committed to a career in services to children.

-- Readily develop rapport with children of all ages.

-- Handle crisis situations in calm and effective manner.

-- Excellent verbal and written communications skills.

-- Hard-working, reliable; able to collaborate in a team effort.

Experience

1986 to Present   Program Coordinator, Family Services, King County
                                     Child Abuse Treatment Program

Child Therapy

-- Conduct individual and group play therapy for preschool children. Designed imaginative play forums as treatment for family-related stress.

Parent Education

-- Collaborate with other therapists in leading concurrent therapy groups for children and their parents. Conduct assessments of family stressors impacting on parents and children. Develop treatment plans addressing the needs of both parent and child. Design activities for supervised parent/child interactions to develop improved family relationships. Provide support and psycho-education for parents at high risk for abuse or neglect of their children, or other family violence.

Crisis Intervention

-- Intervene in cases of child abuse and neglect. Conduct an immediate assessment of risks to the child; collaborate with Social Services Department, other community therapists, and family members to ensure the safety of the child. Intervene in cases of family violence such as spousal abuse and threat of suicide.

1981 to 1986   Staff Therapist/Adoption Worker Family & Children
                                                    Services, Tacoma, WA

Family Therapy

-- Investigated and evaluated more than 450 prospective couples and families for their appropriateness for placement of adoptive children.
-- Developed and implemented support group meetings for adoptive parents, focusing on issues of healthy child-parent relationships.
-- Conducted individual and family therapy sessions.

1980 to 1982 Clinical Social Work Internships

-- Provided individual and group counseling for students at Student Mental Health Center at University of Washington.
-- Conducted individual and group counseling with children 7 to 12 years at the Washington State Mental Health Center in Tacoma.

Education

Master's in Social Work, University of Washington, 1982
Bachelor of Arts, Psychology, University of Washington, 1980

Johnathan Jennings-Krepp
42116 Highway to the Stars
Seattle, WA 98000
206 233-4453 messages

Social Work Supervisor. Program Coordinator. Social Worker.
Counseling. Child Therapist. Family Counselor. Parent Education. Crisis
Intervention. Adoption Worker. Clinical Social Work. Internship. Psycho-
Education. Mental Health. MSW. Bachelor's Degree. Psychology.
University of Washington. Seattle. Tacoma. King County.

Objective:

Social worker position providing counseling to children and their families.

Highlights of Qualifications:

-- More than 5 years' experience working with children and
   their families.

-- Enthusiastically committed to a career in services to
   children.

-- Readily develop rapport with children of all ages.

-- Handle crisis situations in calm and effective manner.

-- Excellent verbal and written communications skills.

-- Hard-working, reliable; able to collaborate in a team effort.

Experience

1986 to Present	Program Coordinator, Family Services, King County Child Abuse Treatment Program

(The rest of this resume remains the same)

Joshua Rubin

7666 MarthaLee Court
Dexter, MO
Telephone: (314) 787-8888

Logistics executive, senior level, with proven ability
to design and manage distribution function. Cutting
edge of industry practices that make major contribution
to profitability. Proven leadership in computer and
quantitative techniques that streamline operations, add
profits.

Experience

1987-Present   **CHICKENTONIGHT FOOD PROCESSING INC.**
                Director of Distribution

- Report to Senior Vice President Operations for
  $1.4 billion corp.

- Direct worldwide corporate warehousing and
  transportation; 9 plants, 650 employees, $110
  million budget.

- Direct computerized order entry/distribution
  planning system permitting strategic
  transportation planning (annual freight savings:
  $25 million).

1978-1987   **REDWING SUDS COMPANY**
                Distribution Manager (1984-1987)

- Reported to Exec. V.P. Operations for this $835
  million bottler of carbonated beverages.

- Managed Corporate Distribution Department (260
  employees, $87 million budget) with nationwide
  distribution network.

- Consolidated field warehousing facilities into 4
  leased regional hub facilities (annual space
  savings of $9.6 million and freight savings of 16%).

- Managed development/implementation of computer
  simulated shipping model (annual freight savings -
  $4.5 million).

Senior Distribution Analyst (1981-1984)

- Reported to Distribution Manager with
  responsibility for conducting several facilities'
  planning and space utilization studies.

- Introduced use of MaxPlan computer simulation
  space planning software, cutting project planning
  time by 59%.

Distribution Analyst (1978-1981)

- Provided support to Senior Distribution Analyst
  and Distribution Manager in wide range of studies
  requiring use of quantitative and computer
  techniques.

Education

M.S., Georgia Institute of Technology, 1978
Major: Industrial Engineering
Weller Scholar (2 years)

B.S., Texas A&M, 1976
Major: Industrial Engineering G.P.A. 3.6/4.0
Judson Oil Company Scholarship (4 years)

Community Leadership

President, Madison Valley Education
Commissioner, Madison County
Chairman, Dads for Kids, Avery Chapter
Coach, Madison Valley Little League

Personal

Age 37
Married, 3 Children
U.S. Citizen
Excellent Health

Joshua Rubin

7666 MarthaLee Court
Dexter, MO
Telephone: 314 787-8888

Keyword   Director of Distribution. Senior VP Operations.
Summary $1.5 Billion Food Processing Corporation.
            Warehousing. Transportation. 650 Employees. $110
            Million Budget. Computerized Order Entry. Distribution
            Planning. Master of Science, Georgia Institute of
            Technology. Bachelor of Science, Texas A&M.

Experience

CHICKENTONIGHT FOOD PROCESSING INC.
1987-Present   Director of Distribution

- Report to Sr. VP Operations for $1.4 billion corp.

- Direct worldwide corporate warehousing and transportation; 9
  plants, 650 employees, $110 million budget.

- Direct computerized order entry/distribution planning system
  permitting strategic transportation planning (annual freight
  savings: $25 million).

REDWING SUDS COMPANY
1978-1987

    Distribution Manager (1984-1987)

- Reported to Exec. V.P. Operations for this $835 million
  bottler of carbonated beverages.

- Managed Corporate Distribution Department (260 employees,
  $87 million budget) with nationwide distribution network.

- Consolidated field warehousing facilities into 4 leased
  regional hub facilities (annual space savings of $9.6
  million and freight savings of 16%).

(The rest of this resume remains the same)

Jason Anson Romero

17452 E. Emile Zola   (602) 345-5552 home
Phoenix, Arizona   (602) 345-2555 message

Summary of Qualifications: More than 10 years' experience as a Systems Engineer and Manager in telecommunications industry.

Objective: Senior systems engineer for television network or news service.

Work Experience:

Copper State Telecommunications   Manager of Systems Engineering
Scottsdale, Arizona   July 1987 to Present

* Researched, identified and developed corrective measures for a series of costly transmission difficulties, which resulted in saving firm more than $1.5 million annually.

* Developed and implemented technical training program for all engineering personnel resulting in cost- and time-saving work procedures of more than $46,000 annually.

* Due, in part, to the above technical training program, firm was awarded "General Excellence in Employee Satisfaction" Award by National Cable Operators Association.

Mogollon Rim Cable Television   Systems Engineer
Heber, Arizona   April 1983 to July 1987

* Designed, constructed and placed into operation this 1,200-customer rural cable television system.
* Wrote and implemented a marketing campaign to motivate technician/installers to sell to individual customers, resulting in a 250% increase in system growth during first 12 months of operation.

Education:
BS, Electrical Engineering   Arizona State University 1982

Jason Anson Romero

17452 E. Emile Zola   602 345-5552 home
Phoenix, Arizona   602 345-2555 message

Keyword Profile: Systems Engineering Manager. Electrical Engineer.
Senior Engineer. Systems Engineer. Television Network. Transmission.
Telecommunications. News Service. Training. Cable Television. National
Cable Operators Association. Technical Writing. BS, Electrical Engineering.

Summary: More than 10 years' experience as a Systems Engineer and
Manager in telecommunications industry.

Objective: Senior systems engineer for a major television network or
news service.

Work Experience:

Copper State Telecommunications   Manager of Systems Engineering
Scottsdale, Arizona   July 1987 to Present

* Researched, identified and developed corrective measures for a
  series of costly transmission difficulties, which resulted in saving firm
  more than $1.5 million annually.
* Developed and implemented technical training program for all
  engineering personnel that resulted in cost- and time-saving work
  procedures.
* Due, in part, to the above technical training program, firm was
  awarded "General Excellence in Employee Satisfaction" Award from
  National Cable Operators Association.

Mogollon Rim Cable Television   Systems Engineer
Heber, Arizona   April 1983 to July 1987

* Designed, constructed and placed into operation this 1,200-customer
  rural cable television system.
* Wrote and implemented a marketing campaign designed to motivate
  technician/installers to sell to individual customers, resulting in a
  250% increase in system growth during first 12 months of operation.

Education:
Bachelor of Science, Electrical Engineering, Arizona State University, 1982

MICHAEL YUBAN
44337 N. Canyon Rd.
Tucson, AZ 85000
(602) 477-0074

Seven years' experience in public relations, marketing communications and advertising. Worked as account executive...promoted to senior account executive with responsibilities that included planning, developing and executing major promotional campaigns. Managed account executive team of five in a leading Phoenix marketing communications firm.

* Responsible for adding 17 new accounts to communications firm's portfolio over four-year period.

* Arranged 7 network television appearances of clients on major news and talk programs.

* Planned, developed and opened branch office in Tucson.

A rainmaking senior account executive who knows how to handle clients A-Z. A proven public relations professional who has personally been responsible for high-value international media exposure for his firm's major clients.

ACCOMPLISHMENTS

* Conceived, developed and executed major promotional campaign for five Fortune 500 companies.

* Recruited and trained a branch office staff of nine, which is responsible for 31 percent of firm's annual billing.

* Personal consultant and advisor for the chief executive officers of two Fortune 500 companies.

EXPERIENCE

HONDO LARSON MARKETING COMMUNICATIONS   Manager 1986 to present
Phoenix, Arizona

Responsible for Tucson branch. Annual revenues in mid-six figures. Directly supervised staff of five.

H.R. GRAVES PUBLIC RELATIONS   Sr. Account Executive   1980 to 1986
Phoenix, Arizona

Responsible for 12 major clients. Developed and executed public relations, publicity and promotional campaigns.

ARIZONA DAILY BUGLE   Staff Writer   1974 to 1980
Phoenix, Arizona

Award-winning (Press Club, three years) reporter and feature writer for statewide daily publication. Primary assignment was the State Capitol, with auxiliary responsibilities in state offices in Tucson, Flagstaff and Yuma.

EDUCATION

Bachelor of Arts, Journalism, University of Arizona, 1974

MICHAEL YUBAN
44337 N. Canyon Rd.
Tucson, AZ 85000
602 477-0074

KEYWORD PROFILE   Public Relations. Marketing. Marketing Communications. Advertising. Account Executive. Senior Account Executive. Writer. Promotional Campaign. Executive Team. Fortune 500. Feature Writer. University of Arizona. Bachelor of Arts. Journalism. Newspaper. Television. Management. Operations. Rainmaker.

Seven years' experience in public relations, marketing communications and advertising. Worked as account executive ... promoted to senior account executive with responsibilities that included planning, developing and executing major promotional campaigns. Managed account executive team of five in a leading Phoenix marketing communications firm.

* Responsible for adding 17 new accounts to communications firm's portfolio over four-year period.

* Arranged 7 network television appearances of clients on major news and talk programs.

* Planned, developed and opened branch office in Tucson.

A rainmaking senior account executive who knows how to handle clients A-Z. A proven public relations professional who has personally been responsible for high-value international media exposure for his firm's major clients.

ACCOMPLISHMENTS

* Conceived, developed and executed major promotional campaign for five Fortune 500 companies.

* Recruited and trained a branch office staff of nine, which is responsible for 31 percent of firm's annual billing.

* Personal consultant and advisor for the chief executive officers of two Fortune 500 companies.

EXPERIENCE

HONDO LARSON MARKETING COMMUNICATIONS   Manager
Phoenix, Arizona   1986 to present

Responsible for Tucson branch. Annual revenues in mid-six
figures. Directly supervised staff of five.

H.R. GRAVES PUBLIC RELATIONS   Sr. Account Executive
Phoenix, Arizona   1980 to 1986

Responsible for 12 major clients. Developed and executed
public relations, publicity and promotional campaigns.

ARIZONA DAILY BUGLE   Staff Writer
Phoenix, Arizona   1974 to 1980

Award-winning (Press Club, three years) reporter and feature
writer for statewide daily publication. Primary assignment was
the State Capitol, with auxiliary responsibilities in state
offices in Tucson, Flagstaff and Yuma.

EDUCATION

Bachelor of Arts, Journalism, University of Arizona, 1974

Author's Comment: As we mentioned earlier, the performance format, strong in itself, does not marry well with a keyword summary. Too many elements compete for the resume reader's eye.

Scott L. Shannon

6343 Baldwin Dr.   Residence: (301) 979-8864
Baltimore, MD 92000   Messages: (301) 979-0876

Objective: Manufacturing Management

Qualifications:

- Profit-oriented executive with more than 12 years' manufacturing managerial experience.

- Documented record in cost-reduction and product improvement.

- Extensive experience in planning and implementation, analytically defining and solving manufacturing problems.

- Proficient in robotic design and programming.

Accomplishments:

- Designed and installed material management system, reducing inventory by more than $5 million (64%) over a two-year period.
- Reduced manufacturing plant's burden by 37 percent in two years, saving $723,000 annually by careful review of company expenditures and JIT personnel utilization.
- Developed and implemented more than 75 cost-reduction and production improvements, resulting in a $62,000 annual savings.
- Reduced material costs with aggressive management of purchasing, resulting in a $43,000 annual savings.

Experience: Director of Manufacturing Pyramid Plastics, Inc., 4 years
                       Director of Manufacturing Precision Toys, Ltd., 5 years
                       Factory Superintendent   Precision Toys, Ltd., 2 years

Education: Bachelor of Science, Manufacturing Engineering, University of Minnesota

Scott L. Shannon

6343 Baldwin Dr.   Residence: 301 979-8864
Baltimore, MD 92000   Messages: 301 979-0876

Keywords:

Manufacturing Management	Director
Manufacturing Problems	Robotics
Programming	Inventory
Bachelor of Science	Design Engineering
University of Minnesota	Material Management
Production	JIT

Qualifications:

- Profit-oriented executive with more than 12 years' manufacturing managerial experience.
- Documented record in cost-reduction and product improvement.
- Extensive experience in planning and implementation, analytically defining and solving manufacturing problems.
- Proficient in robotic design and programming.

Accomplishments:

- Designed and installed material management system, reducing inventory by more than $5 million (64%) over a two-year period.
- Reduced manufacturing plant's burden by 37% in two years, saving $723,000 annually by careful review of company expenditures and JIT personnel utilization.
- Developed and implemented more than 75 cost-reduction and production improvements, resulting in a $62,000 annual savings.
- Reduced material costs with aggressive management of purchasing, resulting in a $43,000 annual savings.

Experience: Director of Manufacturing Pyramid Plastics, Inc., 4 years
             Director of Manufacturing Precision Toys, Ltd., 5 years
             Factory Superintendent   Precision Toys, Ltd., 2 years

Education: BS, Manufacturing Engineering, U. of Minnesota.

6

Resumes by the Dozen

Want a Special Job? Address It by Name in Your Resume

This chapter examines why it's effective to write more than one resume version, even in a digital age when resumes are saved in electronic databases and will pop up when appropriate. You'll find tips here for tailoring your core resume to specific positions.

Max Hart, a men's clothing tycoon, is said to have once summoned his advertising manager to complain that a new advertising campaign was too wordy.

The ad manager dug in his heels and said Hart was wrong. To prove it, the ad manager offered to bet Hart 10 bucks that he could write a whole newspaper page of solid type and that Hart would read every word of it. Hart took the bet.

"I won't have to write a line to win my point," the ad manager boasted with a knowing glint in his eye. "I'll only tell you the headline: *'This page is all about Max Hart.'*"

The behavior illustrated in this simple anecdote goes straight to the heart of ancient psychological precepts: "Start with me and we can talk about you later. Acknowledge me and I'm yours. Tell me I'm special and you can keep me forever."

The magic that happens when you focus on the person you're trying to sell to is the reason great salespeople make it a point to remember names. It's why newspaper people will more readily open press releases addressed to them by name than those addressed to "Business Editor" or "Careers Columnist." It's why all of us are pleased when someone remembers our birthday.

Al Smith, who was governor of New York in the 1930s, once was asked why he signed with a small newspaper syndicate when the giants were dogging his footsteps. Smith replied, "All the guys from the big syndicates told me how great they are; the small syndicate guy told me how great I am."

The principle of turning the spotlight on others—rather than on ourselves—can be applied with great effect in the process of using resumes to get job interviews.

When you tailor your core resume to fit a specific job, you pay the employer the ultimate compliment. Even when the employer recognizes your customized resume as pure strategy, the employer will like it and will like you. Nobody doesn't like being singled out for attention.

HOW TO WRITE A PERSONALIZED RESUME

Until you're on more familiar ground when assembling a resume a computer will read, you may want to get organized.

Begin with a sheet of paper similar to the form shown in Figure 6–1. Use "Help-Wanted Ad Worksheet" as your heading, and set up one worksheet for each ad you plan to answer.

1. Attach the help-wanted ad to the worksheet, and fill in the top lines with company and job information.
2. With a highlighter, mark the contact information and the keywords in the ad.
3. Write down the qualifications you possess—your keywords.
4. Match your keywords to those given in the ad. A computer doesn't care about the order of keywords you use, but a human screener, who perhaps wrote the ad, may find your resume easier to appreciate if it follows the ad's agenda.
5. When filling out the form, jot down a capsule of the job so you'll be able to recall it instantly even though you're applying for dozens of positions.
6. Circle matching keywords that are not quite on the mark. As we discuss below, you should give these a little thought before

deciding you are not qualified. In Figure 6–1 (Ajax, Inc.'s request for a national sales manager), let's say you have four years' experience, not five-plus years.

You may be competing with applicants who have one year's experience five times over, while your experience of four years is richly varied and has well prepared you to handle the job.

7. After going through the process, make your judgment call: Do you have enough of the asked-for essential functions of the job, as reflected in your matching keywords, to justify tailoring a resume? As a memory jog, in case you don't respond immediately to the ad, check yes or no in the upper right-hand corner of the form.

Help-Wanted Ad Worksheet

Customize Resume
Yes ✔ No ____

Employer Name __Ajax, Inc.__   Job Title __National Sales Mgr.__

Job Capsule __Build sales across USA. Medical contacts. Travel.__

__High pay.__

Tape Ad Here, Ad Date/Publication

NATIONAL SALES MANAGER

Fast growing, worldwide medical products company seeking National Sales Manager to build and manage its U.S. sales and distributor network. Direct sales exp in medical products and working with distributors a must. Candidate should have 5+ years of sales exp including some sales management, a college degree & be ready to grow with the company. Outstanding comp package for the right candidate. Extensive U.S. travel. Send resume & salary requirement in confidence to:

AJAX, INC.
P.O. Box 128, Town, USA

3/10
Online Ad Service
USA

My Matching Keywords

1. Medical products
2. Direct sales experience
3. Distributors
4. 4+ years' sales experience
5. Sales management
6. College degree (BA)
7. Travel
8. _____
9. _____
10. _____
11. _____
12. _____
13. _____
14. _____
15. _____
16. _____
17. _____
18. _____

Figure 6–1   Worksheet for Answering Help-Wanted Ads

If you have more than 50 percent of the keyword requirements, it's probably worth the effort to submit a customized resume.

If you have less than a 50 percent match in keywords, send your core resume.

Here's the rationale for this advice. If you've got more than half the keywords (essential functions or requirements) the employer asks for, you've probably got a realistic chance of being considered.

If you're below a 50 percent match, you can at least plant your core resume in the company's applicant tracking system. This may result in a call at a later date for a position more closely matching your qualifications. It's a lottery, but you've got to play to win. No resume in, no resume out.

TIPS FOR MATCHING KEYWORDS

The closer you match keywords—and the more keyword matches you present—the higher your ranking on the computer's short list of candidates.

We want to make it very clear that you gain nothing by lying about your qualifications. As we explained in Chapter 4, getting caught in a lie when technology is standing watch can be very costly on a long-term basis.

Equally important, it's wise to frame your response in a positive light so that a keyword search will not pass you by without a glance. A degree of resourcefulness may be required to shape your keyword response.

The following tips on refinements in handling your keywords are offered to prevent the machine from speeding past your resume.

Your objective is to get spinning computer wheels of fortune to stop at your name, realize you have potential as a candidate, and pull you from storage to a "screening screen" where you can be seen, appreciated, and invited to an interview.

Skills

Suppose that a keyword in the job ad is *computer proficiency necessary,* and you're still struggling to learn how to turn on the machine. Take a community college course on computers before fishing in this pond.

If you're computer semiliterate and the other requirements are a "go," you might try "working toward computer proficiency to add even more strengths to my personal versatility." Again, the computer reaches down and, like a magnet, grabs onto "computer proficiency."

In systems with artificial intelligence, use the asterisk technique (Chapter 4) and a footnote that says you are "attending DOS classes [or Lotus (or whatever) classes]."

Remember, you just want someone with human DNA to lock eyes on your resume.

Suppose an ad says you need experience in *Total Quality Management Systems.* You do not have direct experience but you have related experience and you believe that experience to be transferable. How should you handle this partial matchup? A possible statement: "Have read and studied the concepts of Total Quality Management Systems." An alternative: "I have solid experience strongly related to Total Quality Management Systems."

One way or the other, work the buzzword into your resume or cover letter. Otherwise, the computer is speaking English and you are sending spacegrams in Martian.

Marginal Examples

Some creative efforts to stop the computer at your name may be seen as too slick—but they may work.

The employment scanning industry is too new to make definitive statements about how human screeners will react in particular instances.

Here are two examples that are on the edge and may be interpreted favorably or negatively.

1. You are a newspaper advertising salesperson going after a circulation manager's position. The job requires experience with *paid circulation publications.* You're not fibbing when you give your background, describing how you've been marketing the advertising products of a paid circulation publication. You know the computer will see "paid circulation," and may give you the opportunity to go in front of a decision-making manager and state why you think you'd make a fine circulation manager for the newspaper. The decision maker may see it your way—or may throw you out of the office.

2. You've just retired from or quit a law enforcement agency. You decide to try your hand in the private sector. You'd like to become a director of security for a major bank. One of the keyword descriptors calls for experience in *executive protection.*

   Nearly every police officer who's been through any amount of training has been instructed on how to protect mayors, council members, and visiting VIPs. Maybe you haven't actually done it, but then again, many directors of security haven't either. Describe in your resume your instruction and training in being "qualified to assist in *executive protection* during my tour of duty."

These borderline descriptor techniques may not work every time, but you never know what other aspect of your resume will attract attention and persuade the decision maker to take a closer look at you.

The name of the game is getting someone who can hire you to take a closer look at you.

Unacceptable Fudging

Fantasy fails more often than not, in the hard reality of employment fact checking.

Here's an example of the kind of cagey answer you shouldn't even try to pull off. It will turn on you and bite.

Let's say you see an ad calling for a manufacturing engineer with experience in *"extrusion"* (the forcing of metal or plastic through holes to give it a certain shape). You're an engineer and you know how to do that, but you've never done it and you have to refresh your memory by looking up the word in the dictionary.

You write your resume, throw in a little engineerese, and say you have designed your career using the *"extrusion* process, giving it definite shape to accomplish career goals."

It won't fly.

RESUMES TO USE WHEN YOU TAKE THE INITIATIVE

Our advice on creating resumes that you will hand out in networking or in direct unsolicited application is straightforward.

Study the keyword lists in Chapter 3, add any that are pertinent to your occupation, and put in as many keywords as you reasonably can on your core resume. You are trying to cover all possible bases without looking contrived.

Chances increase daily that your resume will be read by a computer searching somewhere in Corporate America. For most people, learning to tailor a core resume is urgent.

Electronics and the profusion of interactive communication, which *Time* magazine calls "communicopia," are to the 1990s what human networking was the 1980s—perhaps more so.

See the future—and make sure it has you in it.

7

Resume Sample Book

30 Models to Get Past Computers

This chapter offers a collection of resumes that both computers and people will love. They are based on real people, but the names, companies, locations, school facts, and other particulars are altered for privacy. They are shown for format and concept only. Don't overlook the checklist that concludes the chapter.

"What people really want are jobs, and even the best resume doesn't guarantee that," says Daniel J. Harriger, product manager of Abra Cadabra Software, a prominent supplier of human resource software systems.

"But you can't leave home without one," Harriger jokes. He says making your resume scanner-friendly is the 1990s career ticket. Toward that goal, glance over these 30 model resumes we have fashioned around real people, but with a keyword twist. To show variety, they range in length from one to three pages. The model resumes have been reduced to fit on this book size, but they should fit on an $8^1/_2 \times 11$ sheet with generous margins. The type is almost 25 percent larger when seen full size.

Many of the following keyword sample resumes are based on resumes graciously supplied by Mark Gisleson, of Gisleson Writing Services, St. Paul, Minnesota.

SONJA J. PARANELLI
3294 N. Oak Drive, #15
Moses Lake, WA 98000
206 969 4313

Keywords:
Certificate in human resource management. Training and
Development. Professional restaurant manager. Trainer.
Communicator. General Manager. Marketing Manager. Customer
Service. Program Director. Bachelor of Arts. University of Idaho.
Teaching certification. Coaching certification.

Objective:
Professional restaurant manager and trainer seeking to make a
career transition into career field of Human Resources by
utilizing prior experience with youth and community resources,
coupled with documented training and motivational skills.

Summary of Professional Qualifications

- Perceptive manager; can identify and correct problems
  impeding organizational progress and performance.
- Motivationally oriented manager; exceptional training
  skills, track record of producing superb teamwork and
  employee unity.
- Skilled communicator; can establish individual and group
  rapport.

Experience

GOLD RUSH STEAK & RIBS Restaurant   General Manager, 1991-Present
Moses Lake, Washington

- Hired to revitalize franchisee's operations, reassess work
  force and restore employee morale and team spirit.

- Praised by top corporate management for raising worker
  accountability, improving customer service. Train all.

- Within six months, turned around franchisee rankings, going
  from 18th out of 18 restaurants in state to consistent
  number one or two ranking.

KING VALLEY BAR-B-QUE   General Manager, 1989 to 1991
Yakima, Washington

- Trained three assistant managers in computerized scheduling,
  interviewing and hiring techniques. Two have since been
  promoted to general manager at other locations.

- Commended by corporate management for consistently
  developing superior shift managers.

SAM'S KOSHER DELI Restaurant   Dining Room Manager, 1988-1989
Yakima, Washington

- Successfully opened Sam's first restaurant as a member of a five-person management start-up team.

- Interviewed, hired and trained all dining room, bar and reception staff personnel.

- Purchased systems and trained employees on a Micros 4700 cash control system.

- Developed employee handbook for company, still in use.

Education

UNIVERSITY OF CATALINA
Certificate in Human Resource Management, 1994
    3.9 GPA. Focus: Training and Development. Helping develop key competencies that enable individuals to maximize job performance.

UNIVERSITY OF IDAHO
Bachelor of Arts in Health and Physical Education, 1974
Certified to teach and coach, postsecondary level, in two states.

Additional Human Resource Experience

CENTRAL YMCA
Spokane, Washington
Youth Services Officer, 1976 to 1978
- Developed and managed a community counseling program for adolescent girls, expanding program beyond initial inner city targeting to include a suburban office.

MABEL CLARK MEMORIAL CLINIC
Seattle, Washington
Training Counselor, 1975 to 1976
- Developed programs, course and seminars in the areas of health issues for use at high school level, and for instructing teachers on use of these programs.

WANATONDA GIRL SCOUT DISTRICT, Seattle, Washington
Program Director - Camping, 1974 to 1976

Examples of Awards

- 1992 REGIONAL GENERAL MANAGER'S TOP EMPLOYEE, Seattle.
- 1990 PRESIDENT'S AWARD - KVBBQ Corporate: For outstanding achievement in sales performance, customer satisfaction and management innovation.

SEAN MICHAEL GLENN
1225 E. Maple St.
Des Moines, IA 50000
515 676 9355

KEYWORDS Physical Plant Director. Physical Plant Manager. Chief Engineer. Operations. Plant Maintenance. Construction. Security Systems. HVAC. Chief Power Plant Engineer. Stationary Engineer. OSHA Standards. Chief Engineer's License.

OBJECTIVE Physical Plant Director or Manager in private sector where experience-based competence is needed.

EXPERIENCE

HAWKEYE CORRECTIONAL FACILITY, Ankeny, Iowa
Physical Plant Director, November 1989 to Present

-- Started up the Engineering Department, writing all maintenance staff position descriptions, determining work hours and rules, as well as the number of staff required to maintain the institution.

-- Developed hiring schedule for staff as the new facility was opened, and hired all maintenance staff.

-- Direct the operation, installation, and maintenance of the HVAC and security systems, and all other new equipment.

-- Developed initial budget requirements; forecast biennial budgets.

-- Worked with the Division New Building Construction, a Des Moines architectural firm, and construction companies during the building of the new maximum security institution.

-- Took a leadership role in all phases of a recent 83,000 sq. ft. expansion project.

IOWA WOMEN'S CORRECTIONAL FACILITY, Corydon, Iowa
Acting Physical Plant Director, September 1981 to October 1989

-- Supervised the operation, maintenance, and repair of all buildings, systems, and grounds.

-- Directed the work of the power plant, building maintenance department, water treatment plant, ground personnel, and fire and safety office.

-- Assisted in the planning and programming of major repairs, remodeling and new construction throughout the institution.

-- Formulated and presented operational budget for activities personally supervised.

Chief Power Plant Engineer, September 1974 to August 1981

-- Supervised stationary engineers, water treatment plant supervisor, ground maintenance crew, planning and prioritizing work flow.

-- Wrote job descriptions; developed preventive maintenance program for the power plant.

-- Prepared monthly, quarterly and yearly reports.

-- Filled in for the plant operations director and other positions as necessary.

-- Supervised private contractors during major renovation projects.

-- Developed financial statements, projected capital appropriation requests.

Assistant Chief Power Plant Engineer, June 1973 to September 1974

-- Supervised stationary engineers.

-- Prepared quarterly and yearly reports; maintained payroll records for stationary engineers, water treatment plant supervisor and other personnel.

-- Provided documentation and input for financial statements and future capital improvement appropriation requests.

COMMITTEE EXPERTISE

STATE of IOWA -- DEPARTMENT OF ADMINISTRATION
Refrigeration and Air Conditioning Advisory Standards and Value Improvements Committees, 1976 to 1977.

Actively participated in efforts to standardize and ensure quality of parts and equipment for refrigeration and air conditioning purchased for the State of Iowa, in conjunction with the Division of Procurement.

STATE OF IOWA -- DEPARTMENT OF CORRECTIONS
Engineering and Plant Maintenance Committee, 1979 to 1980.

Consultant Task Force for development of heating, ventilating and air conditioning systems for state institutions.

Engineering and Plant Maintenance Committee, 1976 to 1977

Chaired a consultant task force responsible for development of heating, ventilating and air conditioning system at Windsor Heights Maximum Security Facility.

SOUTHERN IOWA CORRECTIONAL FACILITY, Centerville, Iowa
Engineering and Plant Maintenance Committee, 1977 to 1980

   Chaired the renovation of existing facility to medium
   security institution status.

Safety Committee, 1974 to 1980

   Developed and determined safety precaution to be used in
   industrial work areas, making visual checks to ensure
   compliance with OSHA standards.

Pay Plan Committee, 1977 to 1980

   Developed wage scales, set criteria for wage advancement for
   more than 800 facility workers.

   Developed specification for amount, size and heat content
   for coal burnt each fiscal year.

PROFESSIONAL AFFILIATION

HAWKEYE STATE CHIEF ENGINEERS GUILD
     President, 1982-84
     Board of Directors, 1981 to Present

LICENSURE

   Chief Engineers License, Grade A

EDUCATION

DES MOINES TECHNICAL COLLEGE, Des Moines, Iowa
Undergraduate Studies

CONTINUING PROFESSIONAL EDUCATION
Courses, Seminars and Workshops - 1980 to present

     Managing Change-Diversity in Workplace
     Drug Identification Training
     Powerful Writing Skills
     Energy Conservation
     Quality Emphasis Management
     Ethics in Action
     Facilities Management
     Safety Training Observation Program
     Hiring and Firing
     Selection Interviewing
     How to Manage Multiple Priorities
     How to Manage Projects
     Personal Time Management for Professional-Technical Staff
     Dale Carnegie-Effective Speaking and Human Relations
      Outstanding Performance Award

MICHELLE ANDREA HANCOCK
6693 Camino del Sol
Springfield, MA 92000
Residence: 413 289 5917

KEYWORD SUMMARY

Dental Lab Professional. Certified Dental Technician. Crown Technician. Bridge Technician. Implant. Stryker Sustain. Anchor. Vident. Implant Support Systems. Hall Staple Implants. Core-Vent. Branemark. Sterioss Implant Systems. Interpore.

PROFESSIONAL SUMMARY

Highly skilled professional with more than 15 years' dental field experience. Excellent technical skills and knowledge of implants. Works and communicates well with dentists. Experienced in giving on-site briefing and instructions to doctors one-on-one, or in groups of up to 70. Work with audio-visual presentations, as a member of a team or independently.

EXPERIENCE

Bay Water Dental Service, Inc.

1991 - Present   IMPLANT DEPARTMENT MANAGER, Milford, MA

- Reorganized the Crown & Bridge department, starting a new 20-person department specializing in implants and related work only. Strong first-year growth: 31% of business.
- Work with as many as 45 dentists daily over the telephone regarding design, procedures and costs.
- Estimate overall project costs and time requirements for developing needed refinements to existing procedures.
- Know all current dental lab systems, methodologies, products.

1987 - 1991   CROWN & BRIDGE MANAGER

- Managed 12 employees engaged in various aspects of crown and bridge production and implant dentistry.
- Trained or supervised training of employees in production areas, client relations and development of effective time management skills.
- Provided and directed telephone support to dentists and staff in response to technical questions and procedural issues.

Royal Dental Services

1985 - 1986   CROWN & BRIDGE TECHNICIAN. Newton, MA

- Waxing
- Finishing metal
- Casting
- Investing

Jacobson Dental Services, Inc.

1975 - 1985   CROWN & BRIDGE TECHNICIAN. Worcester, MA

- Work responsibilities and training included waxing, 1980 to 1985, finishing metal, casting and investing, 1976 to 1980.

EDUCATION

National Dental Technician College
Worcester, MA
Certified Dental Technician, 1985

CONTINUING PROFESSIONAL EDUCATION

- Comply with all continuing education requirements necessary for maintaining Certified Dental Technician-CDT designation.
- Ongoing in-house training, focusing on implant technology, lab procedures and maintaining quality client relations.
- Participate in annual Massachusetts Dental Laboratory meetings.

JOSHUA JACOB MURPHY
2222 Norcroft Lane
Lincoln, NE 68000
308 579 2101

Hospitality Professional. Hotel manager. Hospitality management. Sales. Marketing. Assistant General Manager. General Manager. Director of Guest Services. BS. University of Washington. Hotel Management Degree.

Qualified by 10 years of increasingly responsible positions in the hospitality industry, with a bachelor's degree in hotel management.

Specific Responsibilities Included:

Hotel Management	Guest Relations Campaigns
Sales Forecasting	Marketing Presentations
Market Research	Advertising
Training	Community Leadership

PROFESSIONAL EXPERIENCE

St. Regis Hotel & Resort, Lincoln, Neb.   1991-1994

Assistant General Manager

RESPONSIBILITIES

At 340-suite luxury hotel with 3,500 sq. ft. of banquet facilities, had responsibility for all facets of daily hotel operations. Oversaw all department managers, supervisors and over 100 full- and part-time employees to ensure the delivery of consistently superior service.

Full responsibility for sales and marketing, advertising strategies, guest relations campaign, employee training.

Represented hotel at various civic and community functions and meetings, contributing expertise and resources to maintain positive public image and effective community relations.

RESULTS

- Achieved record occupancy rate and banquet sales over a four-year period with an average vacancy rate of 10% versus an industry average of 33%.

- Guest relations campaign so successful it was adopted companywide, 18 cities.

- For employee training program, received recognition and cash award from senior management for improved morale and reduced turnover.

Missouri Manor & Convention Center, Kansas City, Mo. 1988 - 1991

Director of Guest Services

RESPONSIBILITIES

> At 700-room convention center with 33,000 sq. ft. of banquet
> facilities, and a health club, supervised a staff of 65
> employees responsible for all guest services including those
> related to such special events and convention activities as:
>
> - The World Series   - Super Bowl XXVII
> - NCAA Basketball Tournament - NCAA Track & Field Meet

Night Assistant Manager   1985 - 1988

- Supervised front office, housekeeping, food & beverage staff
  and supervisors. Received extensive sales & marketing
  training.

RESULTS

- Guest stays extended by 8% over two years. Hotel manager
  credits my successful guest relations policies.
- Banquet facility profit up by 25 percent during my watch.

EDUCATION

Bachelor of Science in Hotel Management, 1984
University of Washington, Seattle, Washington

Additional Continuing Education in various courses and seminars:
Missouri Valley Lodging Association management, interviewing,
hiring and training seminars; State of Missouri Techniques in
Alcohol Management - TAM Licensing, Workers' Compensation,
Unemployment Law, Labor Relations.

AFFILIATIONS

Cornhusker Chamber of Commerce   1992 to Present
Jackson Community College Advisory Council   1986 to Present
Hotel Sales & Marketing Association   1982 to Present
Nebraska Hotel Motel Association   1993
Greater Kansas City Chamber of Commerce   1985 to 1994

COMMUNITY

Chair, United Way "Spirit of Missouri" fundraiser   1993
Lancaster County Youth League Sports Programs 1992 to Present
Missouri Valley Big Brothers-Big Sisters Program   1984

LEE ANN JAMESON

865 Oaklane Drive
Mobile, AL 31000
205 729-4208

KEYWORDS. Real Estate Attorney. Real Estate Law. Strategic Planning. Land Use Planning. Negotiation. Analytical Abilities. Mortgage Lender. Mortgage Finance. Production Director. Research Director. Residential Real Estate Practice. American Bar Association. State Bar Association. City Bar Association. Master's Degree. Juris Doctor. Bachelor's Degree in Economics. Yale University. University of Alabama. University of Mississippi.

SUMMARY

- Successful attorney with solid real estate law track record.

- Successful in strategic planning and implementation.

- Successful record of cost-effective solutions.

- Broad background in real estate.

- Highly skilled communication, negotiation and analytical abilities.

EXPERIENCE

CONFEDERATE MORTGAGE COMPANY, INC., Atlanta, Georgia
Leading residential mortgage lender throughout the southeastern
United States; $16 billion in mortgage originations in 1994.

Director of Production, Policy & Analysis   1992 - Present
Reporting to the Senior Vice President

- Create and develop a highly effective quality management team responsible for production efficiency, closing policy, planning and vendor management.

- Lead major initiative drive to improve the closing process through automation with projected annual cost savings of $487,000.

- Initiate and implement creative solutions to successfully improve production efficiency and customer satisfaction; achieved an 86 percent reduction in closing errors and an 18 percent improvement in customer satisfaction in 1993-94.

- Facilitate strategic planning process of key departments, resulting in new initiatives to achieve company goals.

Research Director   1990 - 1992

- Researched and analyzed federal and state mortgage banking statutes and regulations; monitored legislation and participated in implementation, resulting in a strong record of compliance.

- Performed as company expert in state and federal law compliance.

- Obtained mortgage banker licenses and completed detailed annual reports for regulatory agencies.

JUDGE THOMAS SILAS MARNER, Atlanta, Georgia
Law Clerk 1988 to 1990

- Provided general legal research to legal department in the areas of federal and state mortgage and real estate related laws.

- Created an efficient system to update and maintain a compilation of state and federal law requirements.

BOW, BEAUREGARD & JACKSON
Paralegal Summers, 1986 to 1987

- Drafted contracts, pleadings and legislation; researched and wrote briefs and memoranda; performed real estate title searches.

EDUCATION

YALE UNIVERSITY
Juris Doctor, cum laude 1987
HONORS: Dean's List; Finalist, Appellate Advocacy Competition.

UNIVERSITY OF ALABAMA
Master's Degree in Strategic Planning-Land Use Planning 1990

UNIVERSITY OF MISSISSIPPI
Bachelor of Arts in Economics 1984

INTERNSHIP

OFFICE OF THE STATE AUDITOR, Jackson, Miss.
Intern 1985

- Performed financial analyses of Mississippi cities and counties, including public enterprises.

AFFILIATIONS

American Bar Association - Real Estate, Probate, and Public Law sections
Mississippi Bar Association
Florida Bar Association
Alabama Bar Association
Greater Mobile Bar Association

ROBERT JARED KLEIN
1010 Farley Way
Fresno, CA 93000
415 324-0967

KEYWORDS

Transportation Management Professional. General Manager. Assistant General Manager. Regional Distribution. Manager. Supervise Drivers. Supervise Personnel Functions. Workers' Compensation. Inbound Operations Management. Freight Operations. LCV. Freight Operations Supervisor. Dockworker Supervisor. Dispatch. DOT Regulations. Training. On-Time Delivery. Backhaul Business. Fleet Maintenance. BA Degree in Economics. Fresno State University.

Strengths include:

- Wide experience in trucking
- Good people skills
- Communication skills
- Team player, lead by example
- Bringing in business
- Goal oriented
- Committed to on-time performance
- Troubleshooting

TRANSPORTATION EXPERIENCE

GOLDEN STATE TRUCKING EXPRESS, Fresno, California   1992 to Present
A private management company handling transportation for San Joaquin Valley agricultural industries.

Assistant General Manager

Report directly to General Manager at the Regional Distribution Center in San Francisco. Manager of Fresno and Bakersfield offices with responsibilities for all of Central California and western Nevada.

Supervise 37 drivers. Direct office staff. Do training. Oversee workers' compensation claims, compliance with DOT regulations, longer combination vehicle operations. Supervise incentives and bonuses. Ensure customer satisfaction through on-time delivery.

Solicit backhaul business to maintain revenues and help meet client-set cost-per-unit targets. Monitor and enforce fleet maintenance contract.

KINGSBURG FREIGHTWAYS, Kingsburg, California   1992
Inbound Operations Manager

A common carrier with $96 million in annual revenues.

Reorganized internal route delivery, significantly increasing on-time delivery performance from 75 to 87 percent.

Supervised six dispatchers coordinating a three-shift operation. Supervised up to 16 dockworkers.

FARM-TO-MARKET EXPRESSWAYS, Hanford, California   1988 to 1992
Freight Operations Supervisor

A division of Kingsburg Freightways, Inc.

Trained and developed 75 driver-sales personnel, providing strong leadership in maintaining high productivity and a 93% on-time delivery rate.

Interacted effectively with business customers, providing information and resolving diverse problems -- contributing to an annual growth rate of 23%.

Identified and solved problems with a major account, reducing damage and shortage claims by $450,000, while ensuring continued customer satisfaction by bringing in a new two-year contract.

Planned and scheduled manpower and equipment, making optimal use of labor force while reducing established operating ratio by 25%.

SOUTHERN CALIFORNIA FREIGHTWAYS, Fresno, California   1983 to 1988
Dock Supervisor - Dispatcher

A division of United Treddy Freightways, Inc., with over $1.7 billion in revenues.

Trained 17 drivers-sales personnel, consistently achieving increased individual production. Developed an effective team with "can do" attitude.

Met and exceeded all on-time service goals for five years.

EDUCATION

Fresno State University, Fresno, California
Bachelor of Arts Degree in Economics, 1986

DUDLEY S. GRAVES
7230 North Bend Drive
Phoenix, AZ 85000
602 288-6556

KEYWORDS: Police Officer. Skilled Negotiator. Police Department. Community Relations. Crisis. Emergency. Disaster. Law Enforcement Skills. Bachelor of Arts in Criminal Justice. Arizona State University.

PROFILE

- **Communication:** Proven exceptional written, verbal and presentation skills.
- **Negotiation:** Skilled in negotiation, able to resolve differences.
- **Team Work:** Track record of strong interpersonal skills, with extensive experience in successfully working with administrative-organization procedures and channels.
- **Resourcefulness:** Demonstrated record of overcoming obstacles to get job done; am results-oriented individual.

EXPERIENCE

CAVE CITY POLICE DEPARTMENT, Cave City, Ariz.

Police Officer   **May 1, 1991 to Present**

- Respond to emergency calls involving accidents, natural disasters and other crisis situations, administering medical care.
- Encourage positive community relations through public service and law enforcement.
- Resolve civil disturbance and domestic abuse incidents through advanced negotiating and conflict resolution skills.
- Write and prepare reports, and appear in court.
- Public relations activities include school visits, speaking to community groups and organizations.

Community Service Officer   **January 14, 1991 to May 1, 1991**

- Duties included administrative support, assisting motorists and positive community relations.

EDUCATION

Arizona State University - **Bachelor of Arts, Criminal Justice, 1990**

COLLEGE EMPLOYMENT

Great Western Patrol, Tempe, AZ, Patrol Officer, 1988 to 1991. Arizona State University Security, Tempe, AZ, Patrol Officer, 1986-1990.

COMMUNITY SERVICE

Boy Scouts of America, Greater Tempe Council, Scoutmaster, 1988 - 1991

GEORGE M. CAIN

9430 So. Ashe Street   Salt Lake City, UT 93000   801 324-9006

KEYWORDS   Safety Professional. Safety Consultant. Occupational
              Safety & Health Administration. Accident Prevention.
              Compliance with Federal and State Laws. Claims
              Management. Return-to-work Programs. Insurance.
              Professional Society of Safety. OSHA Training
              Institute. Bachelor of Arts Degree. Health. Physical
              Education. BYU.

EXPERIENCE   SAFETY CONSULTANT, Salt Lake City   1980 to Present

              Assist businesses with the prevention of avoidable
              accidents, analyzing the work environment and work
              practices to lower frequency and severity of accidents,
              and increase productivity. Inspect and bring client
              facilities into full compliance with federal and state
              laws, resulting in lower client insurance claims.

              Review and analysis of insurance. Prepare OSHA reports.
              On-site investigation of accidents-incidents. Training
              employees. Developing return-to-work programs. Handling
              claims management. Preparing materials for inclusion in
              company newsletters. Monitoring of supervisory and
              production personnel. Instituting wellness programs-
              health promotion. Developing procedures for accurate
              documentation of safety incidents.

              Currently work with numerous Utah-based clients, such
              as Gull City Packaging, Levi Die, and Bee State
              Compensation.

EDUCATION   Brigham Young University
              Bachelor of Arts Degree in Health-Physical Education,
              1978

CONTINUING   Membership chair of the Professional Society of
EDUCATION   Safety, 1990 to 1994.
              Certified by the OSHA Training Institute on Voluntary
              Compliance in Safety & Health, 1981.
              Ongoing use and study of PCs and applications in IBM
              and Macintosh environments.

DESIGNATIONS Safety Professional, American Society of Safety
                Engineers
              President, South Salt Lake City Chapter of Toastmasters
              President, Mountain High Business Association

LESLIE ANN STEVENS

3221 Flemming Avenue
Manhattan, Kansas 44000

Home: 913 654-3425
Message:913 385-5959

KEYWORD SUMMARY: Criminal Law. Certified Student Attorney. Top 10%. Westlaw. Arraignment. Negotiation. Investigation. Research. Defense. Counsel. Legal. Internship. Legal Writing. Trial Advocacy. Lexis. Real Estate Law Society. Sociology. Economics. Juris Doctorate. J.D. Degree. Kansas University. Dean's List.

OBJECTIVE: A position in Criminal Law.

LEGAL   TOPEKA COUNTY PUBLIC DEFENDER'S OFFICE, Topeka, Kansas. Certified Student Attorney, March 1993 to Present

Provide legal support services working independently and with staff. Handle criminal arraignments and plea negotiations. Conduct investigations and research defenses using Westlaw. Asked to served as Second Chair by lead counsel.

LAWRENCE COUNTY PUBLIC DEFENDER'S OFFICE
Legal Internship, June 1990 to August 1990

Observed and assisted with client counseling and plea bargaining negotiations. Acquired familiarity with judiciary system and procedures.

LEGAL
EDUCATION   UNIVERSITY OF KANSAS SCHOOL of LAW
Lawrence, Kansas   J.D. Degree, May 1994
Graduation June, 1994

Dean's List. Will graduate in top 10% of class. Electives include two courses in Trial Advocacy, as well as Legal Writing and Advocacy. Lexis and Westlaw training. Am Law Journal editor during senior year.

COLLEGE
EDUCATION   KANSAS STATE UNIVERSITY
Manhattan, Kansas
Bachelor of Arts, Sociology, 1991

Dean's List. Top 10% of class. Charter member, UK Pre-Law Society. Scheduled speakers and participated in a campus legal assistance program.

ANITA SUSANNE MOXLEY
4343 102nd Street
Orlando, FL 34000
904 322-1212

Keywords

Chemicals Executive. President. Vice President. Senior Research Director. Grants. New business start-up. Technology Transfers. Multinational Marketing. $630 Million Sales. Microreplication Technology. Granulated Iron Oxide Pigments. Cement Coloring Equipment. Patent Analysis. PhD in Organic Chemistry, University of Colorado. BS Degree, State University of Iowa.

Technology Start-up Specialist

Executive-level manager experienced in new product development and sales for multinational corporation. Familiar with all aspects of business start-up from establishing corporate identity to product development, marketing and sales.

Extensive background in technology transfers and the patent process; recognized expertise in anticipating technological trends. Results-oriented administrator possessing broad spectrum of knowledge necessary to effectively delegate and monitor a complex, multi-level business.

Experience

SPAMTEK CHEMICAL, Ltd., Tampa, FL
President, 1989 to Present.

Hired to establish a company to market and sell granulated iron oxide pigments and dispensing equipment for coloring cement.

Establish all administrative protocols and operational policies. Obtain customers' clearances, select customs and freight brokers, and determine inventory and distribution procedures. Identify U.S. market segments and potential customers, develop marketing strategy.

Manage all sales formalities, screening procedures and questionnaire design and distribution, including trip reports and profiles, follow up, trials, offers and contracts. Directed initial installations, ensured spare parts and maintenance availability, and personally oversaw troubleshooting throughout the start-up phase.

Results   Achieved sales of $421 million in first fiscal year, with sales of $630 million for second year of U.S. operations. Streamlined parent company's time-intensive perpetual inventory system bringing results to current status instead of 60 days behind, creating 17 percent more executive staff time for sales, and realizing $21 million in annual savings.

Correctly identified product limitations requiring the need for equipment modifications at the source, an Argentina manufacturing company. Developed and demonstrated a new color synthesis approach capable of lowering production costs at the consumer end.

Experience   **CAMDEN-FITCHE CORP., Atlanta, Ga.**
Senior Research Director, 1986 to 1989

New product development for this manufacturer of industrial, commercial, health care, and consumer goods produced and marketed worldwide. Areas of professional focus included: market survey design and analysis; effective use of consumer panels; understanding and advancing microreplication technology; technology transfer.

Rapid assimilation and synthesis of new technologies. Development of analytical procedures. Patent analysis and filing preparation. Experiment design and coordination. Strong computer skills. Cost analysis proficiency.

Technical Manager, 1984 to 1986

Assigned to oversee and troubleshoot disposable contact lens development, including full development, piloting and scaling up of a new process. Managed 37 personnel and five supervisors.

Supervisor-Manager, 1978 to 1984

Designed and piloted a complex, multi-step chemical process in 18 months.

Awards   Camden-Fitche Corporation Golden Step Award, in
                  recognition of $30 million in annual sales, plus
                  Circle of Technical Excellence Award, corporate
                  level

                  Biggest Player Company Award to Industry's Best
                  Research and Development Supervisor, 1982; Best
                  Research Chemist, 1979

Patents   Four granted, three pending.

Publications Journal of American Chemical Society
(sampling)   "Chemistry in the Economy"
                      "Entering the Chemical Industry"
                      "The Two Faces of Chemistry"
                      "Chemistry with a Computer"
                      "The Flash of Genius in Organic Chemistry"
                      "A Short History of Chemistry"

                  Journal of The Conference Board
                      "Managing Technology in a Global Landscape"

                  American Management Association Journal
                      "The Practiced Art of a New Technology"

                  Cement Journal
                      "How to Compete When Your Competition Is
                          Backed by a Foreign Government"

Education   University of Colorado
                  Ph.D. in Organic Chemistry, 1977.

                  Duke University
                  Master's in Business Administration, 1968

                  State University of Iowa
                  Bachelor of Science in Chemistry, 1966.

Kathy Anne McDonald

119 Anne St., #13, Greenville, SC 28807
803 677-2121 messages

Editor. Technical Editor. Writer. Technical Writer. Editorial Experience. English Major. Copy Editing. Wire Service. IBM. Macintosh. Microsoft Word. Aldus Pagemaker. Word for Windows. Paintbrush. Tiffany. WordPerfect. MacDraw. MacPaint. Wire Service. Superfund. Hazardous Waste Reports. Environment. BA.

Summary of Experience

More than 25 years of editorial experience, including eight years of copy editing for major wire service, six years of structural editing, five years of technical editing, two years of technical writing, 10 years of journalistic writing, and 10 years of proofreading. Proficient on the IBM-compatible personal computer using Microsoft Windows, Word for Windows, Paintbrush, Tiffany, and WordPerfect; on the Macintosh computer using Microsoft Word, MacDraw, MacPaint, Aldus Pagemaker.

Much work was performed at home while family was growing up. Now interested in full-time employment. Can provide glowing references, solid work samples.

Education

Bachelor's degree in English, University of North Carolina, Raleigh.

Work Experience

Acme Manufacturing Corp., Greenville, SC
   Technical Writer: 3-88 to 8-93
   Prepared user guides for products.

   Technical Editor: 8-87 to 2-88
   Edited various superfund hazardous waste reports.

Grey, Tripler & Dice Associates, Asheville, NC
   Technical Editor: 1-83 to 7-87
   Set up the editing department for an energy and environmental engineering consulting firm. Other responsibilities included editing all reports, proposals, brochures and presentations issued by the firm.

ComputerHall News, Hendersonville, NC
   Copy Editor: 1-81 to 1-83
   Copy edited and proofread, for a weekly computer newspaper.

Greenville Business Tribune, Greenville, SC
   Copy Editor-Editor: 5-76 to 12-85
   Edited, copy edited, proofread, at business newspaper.

MARION C. EVANS

35 Robins Nest Drive
Toledo, OH 53446
419 765-0123

KEYWORDS

Marketing Manager. Buyer. Merchandising Manager. Marketing. Product Development. Promotions. Advertising. Graphics Production. Direct Mail. Media. New Product Introduction. Training. Travel. Wholesale. Bachelor of Arts. Michigan State.

SUMMARY

A marketing manager with in-depth merchandising and product development experience. Employers describe me as a money maker ... and a creative, high-energy problem solver. Excellent at defining and meeting market needs.

PROFESSIONAL EXPERIENCE

TALENT PROFESSIONAL INTERNATIONAL, Cincinnati, OH 1988 to Present
Marketing Manager
Overall creative and financial responsibility to manage and direct four key areas: Wholesale and related businesses, promotions, advertising, visual display, merchandising, and graphics production.

- Created wholesale division product line and systems.
- Doubled company income in three years.
- Initiated and executed in-house graphics production ... saved $150K advertising agency fees annually.
- Executed 1991 corporate image change ... including visual display, retail packaging and promotions.

THE JEFFERSON MINT, Jefferson Center, PA, 1986 - 1988
Program Manager
Developed original artwork in fine porcelain, bronze and pewter from initial concept to direct mail and media promotion. 26 programs plus Christmas catalog each in excess of $2 million in sales. Travel 50% of job.

MILANO CORPORATION, Chicago, IL, 1984 - 1986
Buyer for leading giftware importers
Purchased 20% of company volume. Developed products from idea conception to market placement. Selected product assortments for catalog. Trained national sales force in marketing new product introductions. Traveled extensively overseas, 5 countries, 28 suppliers.

MICHEALS CREATIVE CRAFTS, Chicago, IL, 1983 - 1984
Buyer for 52 stores in 23 national markets
Responsibilities included annual budget programs for sales, inventory and profit.
Created total concept, product assortments and systems for the custom frame,
organizer and stationery shops. Member of new store and operating committee. Lots
of travel.

CRAFTY CRAFTS AND HOBBIES, Northbrook, IL, 1978 - 1983
National Merchandising Manager and Buyer for mid-western chain of 12 stores.
Turnkey responsibility to open 7 stores. Selected products for institutional catalog.
Lots of travel.

EDUCATION

Bachelor of Arts, Michigan State University, 1972
Numerous Professional Seminars; details upon request.

PROFESSIONAL AFFILIATIONS

American Management Association
Women in Management
American Society of Interior Designers
Hobby Industry Association of America

OTHER

Arts, theater, swimming, needlework, music, dance,
painting, photography, power walking, travel

Kelli S. Regan

24395 Bonita Avenue
Rockville, Maryland 97000
301 535-3312

OBJECTIVE: Drafter

KEYWORDS

Blueprint. Process Flow Diagrams. Drafting. Instrumentation Diagrams.
Intergraph Microstation 3.0. Harvard Graphics 3.0. Lotus 1-2-3. Document
Control Files. Quattro Pro. Structural. Engineering. Electrical. Civil.

OBJECTIVE

Seeking a drafter position that will utilize my up-to-date skills for further
advancement in an engineering organization.

DRAFTING SKILLS

- Process Flow Diagrams
- Piping and Instrumentation Diagrams on Intergraph Microstation 3.0
- Charts and graphs using Harvard Graphics 2.6 and 3.0 software
- Charts on Lotus 1-2-3
- Document Control files and documentation on Word Star 6.0 and
  PerForm software
- Maintain bills of materials using Quattro Pro software

WORK HISTORY

Drafter	Maryland Blueprint & Design	1989 - 1993
	Silver Spring, MD	
Drafter	Young Engineering	1986 - 1988
	Wheaton, MD	

EDUCATION AND TRAINING

Hopkins Community College, Baltimore, MD - 1984, Associate of Arts
Degree. Major: Engineering Technology

Kennedy High School, Baltimore, MD - 1981, General Drafting:
Orthographic Projection, Dimensioning, Cross section, Isometrics

Regional Occupation Program, Towson, MD - 1981, Industrial Drafting:
Structural, Electronic, Mechanical, Civil

QUON X. TRAN

3429 E. Second Avenue
Las Vegas, NV 87000 702 445-6172

Mathematics. Management. Mathematical Computation. Probability. Statistics. Numerical Analysis. Computer Programming. Financial Reports. Financial Analyst. Algebra. Geometry. Trigonometry. Calculus. WordPerfect. Basic. Lotus 1-2-3. Fortran. Pascal. National Honor Society. Asian American Student Association. dBase III+. Bachelor of Science. UNLV. 3.6 GPA.

OBJECTIVE: Mathematics management or technically related field.

SPECIAL SKILLS:
Basic, Fortran, Pascal computer languages.
WordPerfect 6.0, Lotus 1-2-3, dBase III+.

EXPERIENCE:
Jan. 1992 to Present -- **Financial Analyst**
Ace of Spades Casino, Las Vegas
> Monitor and analyze casino's weekly receipts and expenses. Prepare financial reports all gross income.

Sept. 1990 to June 1991 -- **Math Tutor**
Math and Computer Lab, UNLV
> Instructed college students in Algebra, Geometry, Trigonometry, Statistics, Calculus.

Sept. 1990 to June 1991 -- **Computer Lab Assistant**
Information System Department, UNLV
> Assisted instructors with class projects and assisted students in computer lab assignments. WordPerfect, VP-Planner, Lotus 1-2-3, dBase III+, Basic Computer Programming.

June 1990 to Sept. 1990 -- **Staff Learning Assistant**
Learning Center, UNLV
> Created database files using dBase III+. Assisted staff with clerical work.

HONORS AND ACTIVITIES:
Member, National Honor Society.
Member, Asian American Student Association.

EDUCATION:
University of Nevada, Las Vegas, 1991
Bachelor of Science, Mathematics
> Emphasis: Mathematical Computation, Application in Problem Solving, Probability-Statistics, Numerical Analysis, and Computer Programming. **3.6 Grade Point Average**, on 4.0 scale.

JAMIE LEE ALEXANDER

114 W. Raven Avenue, Richmond, VA 39200
804 735-6900 home   804 322-1212 messages

Keywords:
Operations Officer. Operations Department. Bank Teller. Head
Teller. General Business. General Accounting. Management.
Payables. Receivables. Tax Reports. Bookkeeping. Bookkeeper.
Associate of Arts Degree. Virginia Commonwealth University.

Objective:
Financial institution position leading up a management career
path ... Am hard worker, fast learner.

Experience:
Seaside State Bank, Richmond, VA
June 1983 to Present
Operations Officer

> Manage five-person staff and all major functions in the
> operations department. Joined bank as a teller. Promoted in
> 1985 to head teller. Promoted to present position in 1990.

Wells Aircraft Maintenance Company, Richmond, VA
August 1981 to May 1983
Bookkeeper

> Managed bookkeeping functions: accounts payable, accounts
> receivable, payroll, tax reports for small general aviation
> maintenance company while attending college full-time.

Education:
Virginia Commonwealth University, Richmond, VA
Associate of Arts Degree, 1983
Major: General Business and Accounting

GREGORY B. MEADOWS

4900 Mercedes Drive
Philadelphia, PA 77667
814 934-5784

KEYWORDS

Small Business President. Business Unit Manager. Marketing Manager. Product Manager. Brand Manager. Field Sales. National Sales Team. $85 million Sales. National Accounts Manager. District Sales Manager. Number One Market Share. Key Account Sales Programs. Joint Venture. Manufacturers Representative Network. Distribution Network.

EXPERIENCE

DOMINICA, INC., PHILADELPHIA, PA   **1987 - Present**

President

Founded and operate a company that provides records management and retention services to hospitals and other health care organizations. The business reached break-even in only nine months and recently has been sold for a profit.

WESTMAN CORPORATION, CONSUMER PACKAGING DIVISION 1969 - 1987

Business Unit Manager - 1978 - 1987

Under division reorganization identified and developed a national team of field sales offices, staff marketing, and a purchasing group. Product profitability and return on investment accountability dictated strong matrix management of engineering, manufacturing and technical functions. Achievements include:

- Increased sales from $50 million to over $85 million. All products reached #1 market share position and profit margins increased every year. Key account sales programs, product innovation, programmed cost reduction and responsive capital spending secured this position.

- Directed product development which resulted in several products becoming industry standards. Two packages received the coveted "Package of the Year" award.

- Took leadership role in evaluating acquisition opportunities and in establishing joint venture-development relationships. One project reduced the new design cost for printed material by 80%.

- Established a system that reduced slow-moving material from an average of $300 thousand to $125 thousand.

Marketing Manager - 1975 - 1978

Managed the pricing, market strategy, sales support and technical direction of a variety of products. A staff group including two product managers were direct reports. Achievements included:

- Developed packaging for snack foods which quickly grew into a $20 million plus business. Identified the opportunity and implemented program which established the canister package for snack chips. Sales reached $19 million in two years and Westman retained a 75% market share. Earned "Package of the Year" award.

- Established a manufacturers' representative and distributor network to enhance sales of specialized "general line" products.

- Coordinated the necessary financial and operations efforts to establish several new plants. Developed programs for just-in-time delivery and quality assurance.

Field Sales - 1971 - 1975

Progressed rapidly from sales representative, to national accounts manager, to district sales manager. Achievements included:

- Doubled sales in first territory in one year to $4 million.

- Made initial penetration of key national accounts (i.e., Winn-Dixie, Palmolive). Winn-Dixie became 100% account and sales grew to $20 million during this period.

EDUCATION

Master's Business Administration
University of Pennsylvania, Wharton, PA - 1971

Bachelor of Arts, Economics
Lawrence University, Erie, PA - 1969

Richard B. Haynesworth III
Certified Public Accountant

1485 N. Basin Court, Chicago, IL 66000
312 213-3345

KEYWORDS: Certified Public Accountant. Revenue Accounting Manager. Finance. Telephone Company. Research. Development. Information Management. Toll Forecasting. Cash Control. Audit. Auditor. Accounting Supervisor. Treasurer.

CAREER HISTORY:

Illinet Telephone System, June 1986 to Present
Revenue Accounting Manager

One of the largest telecommunications companies in Illinois, this firm is engaged in basic telephone service, advanced voice and data equipment and services, research and development, information management, consulting, financial services, equipment manufacturing and maintenance, and wireless communications.

The Revenue Accounting Department is accountable for all revenue reporting, settlement and cash control functions.

Revenue Accounting is the focal point for all revenue analysis and toll forecasting; Cash Control is the audit center for cash processing.

Using state-of-the-art technology, my department is responsible for the implementation of a new Revenue Accounting Information System.

Mitchner, Sullivan and Fritz & Associates, April 1980 to May 1986
Accounting Supervisor

Was responsible for the assistance and guidance of corporate clients' strategic plans, annual detailed budgets, and monitoring and analysis of variances. Directed yearly inventory counts and other special projects. Fulfilled auditing assignments.

HONORS, ACHIEVEMENTS:

Ranked in the top 10% on the Certified Public Accountants' examination, State of Illinois, 1983.

EDUCATION:

University of Illinois, 1979
Bachelor of Science, Accounting and Finance

Thomas A. Harding

ET2, E-5, USN
Division CE, USS Neversail LL-41
FPO-APO San Francisco, 96000-1000
619 789-1212 messages

Electronics Specialist
Available July, 1995

Keywords: Electronics. Electronics Communications. Audio. Video Distribution. Interior Communications. Naval Training Center. Telephone Systems. Amplifier Circuit. TV. Radio. Quality Assurance. Electronic Circuit Assemblies. Electronics Service and Repair. Alarm Systems. Telecommunications. Bio-Medical. Satellite. CET. AAS Degree in Electronics Technology.

Work: Position in electronics communications, service or repair.

School:

- Interior Communications, Class "A" School, Naval Training Center, San Diego. July 1990 to June 1991.

  Course included six weeks of basic electronics theory, and 16 weeks of hands-on training in troubleshooting and repair of amplifier circuits, alarm systems, telephone systems, navigation systems, TV and radio broadcast systems.

- Victor Valley Community College, Victorville, California   1990 Associate in Applied Science Degree, Electronics Technology Top Student in Class, 3.90 Grade Point Average.

Occupational History:

United States Navy, July 1991 to May 1995

Electronics Technician

Duties include repair of and quality assurance of electronic circuit assemblies. Directly comparable to work in civilian electronic products, from office machines to health equipment, and from computer products to telecommunications service.

Certification:

Associate, International Society of Certified Electronics Technicians Certified Electronics Technician, 1990

Categories of Interest: Telecommunications: Phone; Data; Microwave; VSAT. Bio-Medical. Video Distribution: MATV; Antenna; Satellite.

ELIZABETH R. NICKERSON
11712 North Central Avenue
Phoenix, AZ 85000
Residence 602 355-4512 Message 602 355-6521

Ten years' Progressive Aeronautical and Mechanical Engineering Experience. PhD. Master of Science. Bachelor of Science. Stanford University. UCLA. University of California, Los Angeles. Department of Defense. Secret B.I. Clearance. Mechanical Engineering. Spacecraft. AHIP Helicopter. Symbolic Manipulation Program. IBM 3090. VAX. FORTRAN. NASTRAN. UNIX. DOS. Society of Women Engineers. ASME. ASAE.

SUMMARY OF QUALIFICATIONS

Extensive experience in the disciplines of structural and simulation dynamics, structures, aerospace engineering, mechanical engineering, and software application and development.

Demonstrated ability to apply these methodologies to analyze, evaluate, and incorporate design changes to fixed and mobile structures, vehicles and other environments. Department of Defense Top Secret Clearance.

EDUCATION

Doctorate in Aeronautical Engineering, University of California at Los Angeles, 1982

Master of Science in Mechanical Engineering, Stanford University, 1979

Bachelor of Science in Mechanical Engineering, Summa Cum Laude, University of Missouri at Rolla, 1977

PROFESSIONAL EXPERIENCE

- Developed detailed comprehensive element structural models for dynamic and stress analysis with particular expertise to model and evaluate integrated spacecraft and mechanical systems.

- Conceptualized and formulated theoretical model and software for dynamic and aeroelastic response of coupled, rotor-airframe helicopters in high-speed forward flight.

- Participated in vibration test requirements and data reduction for **AHIP** and **YAH-64** helicopters.

Continued

- Applied Symbolic Manipulation Program, SMP, for developing dynamic equations of motion of multibody systems.

- Conducted time simulation studies of complex multibody systems. Programming and computer experience includes developing software on IBM 3090 mainframe, VAX, and PC computers using FORTRAN, NASTRAN DMAP, BASIC, and C languages under DOS and UNIX operating systems.

EMPLOYMENT HISTORY

Lindbergh Space and Defense Corporation
San Jose, California
Staff Engineer, 1987 - Present

Howard Aircraft Corporation
St. Louis, Missouri
Staff Engineer, 1984 - 1987

GeeBee Helicopters
Costa Mesa, California
Technical Staff, 1980 - 1984

MEMBERSHIPS

Society of Women Engineers
   Chair, Committee on Professional Review, 1987 - 1989
   Chair, Annual Meeting, 1990

American Society of Mechanical Engineers
   Chair, Western Region Membership Committee, 1986

American Society of Aeronautical Engineers
   Co-Chair, Professional Standards, 1990-1992
   Chair, Career Transition Committee, 1993 - Present

OTHER

Prefer technical discipline to management tasks ... Enjoy working with cutting edge technology ... Hobby is training physicians at Western General Hospital to use voice recognition computer system--Kurzweil--to dictate medical record reports ... Another hobby: growing orchids ... Like sports and crossword puzzles ... and a good joke.

STEPHEN J. STERLING

19917 Keeaumoku St.   •   Honolulu, HI 98000   •   808 721-7211

KEYWORDS   Purchasing Manager. Purchasing Supervisor.
Purchasing Agent. Industrial Buyer. Supply
Manager. CPM. NAPM. Procurement. Electronic
Components. Raw Materials. Material Rejection
Board. RFQ.

SUMMARY   Purchasing agent and manager for a number of
mid- to large-size manufacturing firms for the
past 10 years. Seasoned professional who knows how
to buy right.

PROFESSIONAL EXPERIENCE

1986-Present   **Purchasing Manager**
CHEETUM INDUSTRIES, Pearl City, Hawaii.

Supervise the purchase of $12,000,000 materials
annually. Manage staff of two buyers.

• Direct procurement of electronic components, raw
materials, machine parts, plastics and
sub-assemblies. Purchase sheet metal, hot and cold
rolled steels, round tubing and flat bar. Buy
tooling and outside processing services.

• Have saved company $2,000,000 annually since
1987, based on extrapolations of purchasing costs
prior to my assuming the responsibility. Corporate
controller will confirm, after hiring action.
Work closely with vendors by phone and site visits
to ensure quality control and adherence to
delivery schedules.

• Responsible for correct formal Request for
Quotes.

• Negotiate price and best delivery to
substantiate award.

• Conduct and evaluate vendor surveys.

• Attend Material Rejection Board meetings to
discuss rejected parts. Contact vendors to correct
discrepancies or non-conformities.

(Continued)

1980-1986   **Buyer**
                   KAAPIOLANI AERONAUTICS, Honolulu, Hawaii

                   Responsible for the timely ordering, delivery and
                   procurement of flight parts, materials, and
                   hardware to the latest revision pertaining to the
                   program assigned.

                   Daily interfacing with engineers on various
                   projects. Extract part information from blueprints
                   and purchase necessary items. Contact vendors and
                   negotiate prices, receive quotes, issue purchase
                   orders and send to accounts payable department.
                   Keep all information logged and updated on
                   computer. Attend weekly meetings with engineers to
                   update status of project. Procure special
                   processes for parts, including chemical treatment,
                   heat and paint processes. Familiar with military
                   specifications.

1978-1980   **Expeditor**
                   BIG KAHUNA MERCANTILE, Honolulu, Hawaii

                   Responsible for the daily pick-up and delivery of
                   stock transfers, paperwork and supplies for 14
                   different store locations. Kept daily log of all
                   transactions interfaced with on a daily basis.
                   Responsible for mileage tracking and full
                   maintenance of company car.

EDUCATION

   *   Hawaii State University
                   Bachelor in Business

OTHER QUALIFICATIONS

Have earned the title of Certified Purchasing Manager, awarded by
the National Association of Purchasing Management. I have passed
all four examinations with high marks and met the requirements of
experience and education.

* Will complete in 1995.

Terrance A. Thompson

201 Larkspur Lane
Pleasant Valley, NY 15000
518 675-1212

KEYWORDS: Child Care. Teacher. Early Childhood Development. Mathematics Teacher. Private School. Day Care Center. Primary Age Students. Natural Science. Reading. Drawing. Elementary. Education. MA Degree. BA Degree. San Diego State University. University of New Mexico. Doctoral Student.

OBJECTIVE: Position in child care or teaching at a university observational school or day care center -- preferably at a school where I can complete my doctorate in Early Childhood Development.

SUMMARY OF QUALIFICATIONS: Successful with the challenge of teaching groups of children. Patient, confident, and committed in working with children. Teaching credentials in three states: New York, New Jersey and Pennsylvania.

TEACHING EXPERIENCES: Taught junior-high age students in all mathematics subjects; taught math to primary-age students; tutored teenagers in natural science subjects. Supervised 4- and 5-year-old children, teaching them basic skills in reading and drawing.

EMPLOYMENT HISTORY:
1992 to present -- Hilltop Middle School, New Rochelle, NY
1988 to 1992   -- Larkspur Elementary School, Albany, NY
1985 to 1988   -- Madison Junior High, Pittsburgh, PA
1982 to 1985   -- Duke Elementary School, Hackensack, NJ

EDUCATION & CREDENTIALS:

1994 -- Ed.D Studies, two years, Rutgers University
1982 -- Master of Arts, Education, University of Pennsylvania
1980 -- Bachelor of Arts, Education, University of Pennsylvania
Fully credentialed in the states of New York, New Jersey and Pennsylvania.

Rosalee Ann Flowers
12231 S. Lancaster Way
Dallas, TX 75000
214 523-5552

Keywords

Health Maintenance Organization. Member Relations Manager.
Mediator. Moderator. Facilitator. Marriage Counselor. Family
Counselor. Patient Advocate. Elder Care Counselor. MA Degree. BA
Degree. University of Texas. Southern Methodist University.

Objective-Summary

Member Relations Manager's position for a large health
maintenance organization. Have extensive experience with patient
advocacy, as well as supervisory background in agency work. Have
demonstrated competence in coordinating programs. Excellent
mediator, moderator and facilitator. Licensed Marriage and Family
Counselor.

Qualifications

--   Served as patient advocate for two years at community
     clinic.

--   Taught and supervised 12 student teachers.

--   Supervised five employees in my own firm.

--   Mediated domestic conflicts as marriage counselor for 10
     years.

--   Counselor and grievance liaison at mental health agency.

Professional Experience

1982 to Present --   Lone Star Elder Care Referral Service
                     Dallas, Texas - Counselor-Owner

1980 to 1982   --   Women's Resource Center
                     Arlington, Texas - Coordinator for Career Program

1977 to 1980   --   Estrella Mental Health Association
                     Fort Worth, Texas - Teacher-Trainer

Education

Master of Arts, Counseling, University of Texas, 1977
Bachelor of Arts; Marriage, Family & Child Counseling
Southern Methodist University, 1975

GERALD H. COTTON

1111 Central Ave.
Laramie, WY 81000
307 956-1018

KEYWORDS   Reporter. Staff Writer. Feature Writer. Daily
                     Newspaper. News Bureau Manager. Managing
                     Editor. AgriBusiness. Magazine. B.A. in
                     Journalism. State University.

OBJECTIVE   Reporting or Feature-Writing Staff position
                     on 100,000-plus daily newspaper, preferably
                     west of the Mississippi River.

PROFESSIONAL EXPERIENCE

1988 to Present   University News Bureau Manager
                     UNIVERSITY OF WYOMING, Laramie.

                     Supervise staff of four. Generate news of
                     university activities and students for
                     publication on campus as well as weekly and
                     daily publications throughout region.

                     • Redesigned format for campus newspaper
                     • Advise Student Newspaper staff on-campus

1983 to 1988   Managing Editor,
                     GREEN CREEK WEEKLY GAZETTE, Green Creek, WY

                     Hired as a reporter, promoted to managing
                     editor's chair in 1985. This 3,200 weekly
                     circulation newspaper covers all of Box Butte
                     County. Editing and writing duties included
                     all aspects of news and feature reporting.

                     • Developed monthly AgriBusiness Magazine.
                     • Developed and supervised student internships.
                     • Won five state press club awards for
                       writing-editing.

1980 to 1983   Staff Writer,
                     LOGAN DAILY NEWS, Logan, Utah

                     While attending school worked as full-time
                     reporter and feature writer on this 18,000
                     circulation suburban daily newspaper.

EDUCATION

1982   Bachelor of Arts Degree, Journalism,
                     Utah State University

JOHN ANDREW STARK

2121 Avenue J
Denver, CO 84000
303 724-4712

KEYWORDS

Physical Therapy. Physical Therapy Aide. Hospital Aide. UAP staff. Human Anatomy. Human Physiology. Children with Disabilities. Aquatic Routine. BA Biology. University of Colorado.

GOAL

Seeking a position as a Physical Therapy Aide. Wish to work at a hospital in unlicensed assistive personnel pool. My long-term goal is to become a registered physical therapist. Service to others is the keystone of my life.

EDUCATION

Hold a Bachelor of Arts degree in Biology, concentrating on human anatomy and human physiology, from the University of Colorado 1989.

RELEVANT EXPERIENCE

--   Serviced as a physical therapy aide working with children with serious disabilities; performed basic physical therapy routines to facilitate physical development.

--   Implemented adaptive aquatic routines with an adult who is physically disabled.

--   Assisted in supervising recreation activities of children and adults who have mild to severe mental retardation, as volunteer at city-sponsored specialized recreation program.

--   Instructed basic academic subjects in classroom for learning-delayed children.

--   Recorded academic performance of special-education children.

EMPLOYMENT HISTORY

1989 to present -- Teacher,
Collinwood Day School, Brighton, CO

1985 to 1989 -- Personal Care Attendant,
Morgan Senior Care Homes, Boulder.

1980 to 1985 -- Instructional Assistant
Denver County Public School District

Mary Lou Kendell
1521 W. Oceanview Place
Sea Island, GA 40100
912 245-1212

Ready to Be Director of Training and Development

Trainer. Training Director. Training Consultant. Standup Trainer. Curriculum Designer. Financial Training. Technical Skills Training.

Computer-Based Training. Interactive Video. Soft-Skills Training. Interaction Skills. Workplace Attitude Training. Diversity Training. Adult Learning. Group Training. Group Facilitator. Needs Assessment.

Application of Adult Education Theory. Master's Degree. University of North Carolina.

SUMMARY

Extensive corporate experience specializing in training and development, project management and financial analysis training. Am high-energy professional who understands that acquired skills and abilities have become the pivotal resource ... now that human resources account for more than 80% of the Nation's total economic output.

WORK HISTORY

1989 to Present   **Training Director**
Keep Working Temporaries, Brunswick, GA
The leading temporary services firm in city.

- Supervise training of all personnel. Have overseen training of more than 12,000 workers in five years. In addition, provide personal standup diversity training to 14 corporate clients.

- Responsibilities include computer-based training, interactive video and group training. Created 58 needs assessments for corporate clients. Handle both technical and soft-skills instruction.

Continued

- Suggested corporate policy, now adopted: "New skills are needed to match each generation of electronic wizardry."

1987 to 1989   **Training Consultant**
                    Peach State Bank, Waycross, Ga.

- Initiated start-up functions for needs analysis and development of 28 training programs.

- Created program for development, scheduling and delivery of 34 in-house training courses.

1984 to 1987   **Training Manager**
                    Barron's Organization Development Inc.
                    Jacksonville, Fla.

- Interface with finance-oriented users.

- Evaluation and selection of financial software packages; provided support for system software.

- Automated human resource management system to support benefits planning functions.

1982 to 1984   **Trainer**
                    Fields Training Services Inc., Jacksonville, FL

- Gained overview of training field through many temporary assignments for variety of clients.

EDUCATION

1982   Master's Degree, Education
                    University of North Carolina, Asheville

1980   Bachelor of Science, Accounting
                    Troy State University, Troy, Alabama.

Brent B. Burke
2211 Corless Ave.
Kearney, NE 68000
308 224-3312

KEYWORD SUMMARY

Ten years' steadily upward experience in
software engineering. Software Engineer.
Senior Software Engineer. Computer Science.
C. FORTRAN. NCR's VRX. DOS 6.0. DOS/VSE.
Assembly. Z80. HP 9000. Unix. Optical
Computer. Logic Analyzer. Microprocessor.
Company Achievement Award. Motorola. BS.
Mathematics. University Nebraska.

QUALIFICATIONS

• Designed and maintained code for 14
  real-time embedded systems.

• Competent with 12 computer languages,
  including assembly, FORTRAN, and C.

• Competent with 8 operating systems,
  including UNIX, and NCR's VRX.

PROFESSIONAL EXPERIENCE

1989 - 1994   Senior Software Engineer
                Midwest Datacorp, Broken Bow,
                Nebraska

Enhanced, coded, tested, and maintained
real-time embedded system software for two of
company's microfiche machines. Consulted in
installation of companywide software
packages. Developed new standards and
procedures for systems and operational areas.
Received company achievement award, 1991.

-More-

1986 - 1988   Software Engineer
                 Acme Micro System, Kearney,
                 Nebraska

Developed and implemented projects to handle
voice synthesis for real-time system on a
microprocessor. Designed code to handle
voltage modulation. Used Logic Analyzer to
debug and design programs. Documented and
designed a software package for database
management.

1982 - 1986   Software Engineer
                 National Cash Corporation,
                 Madison, Wisconsin

Designed, tested and enhanced an emulator
using 32-bit assembly language (similar to
MC68000). This code was designed for an
on-line, multi-user environment. Used logic
analyzer to debug code. Was a member of a
firmware development group. Used VRX
operating system, and optical computers.

EDUCATION

Have completed 15 hours graduate-level
computer science courses
University of Nebraska, Kearney.

Bachelor of Science in Mathematics, minor in
Computer Science
University of Nebraska, Lincoln.

PERSONAL

- Past president of Junior Achievement
  --Broken Bow, Nebraska--1990

- Past program chair of Association of Local
  Area Network Supporters--Broken Bow,
  Nebraska--1991

- Professional Sector Chair of American Red
  Cross--Kearney, Nebraska--1987, 1988

- Big Brothers Association--Kearney,
  Nebraska--1987-1988

GERALD E. RAINES
238 Hillside Avenue
Yonkers, NY 10703
914 444-1500
914 444-4387 messages

KEYWORDS

MBA. Finance. Top 25% Class. New York University. Sigma Iota Epsilon. MBA Association. Computer Information Systems. Capital Budgeting. Cash Disbursement. Cash Management. Corporate Finance. Financial Planning. Financial Analysis. Float Analysis. Forecasting.

Burroughs Mainframe. COBOL. BASIC. DBASE. EXCEL. Lotus 1-2-3. WordPerfect 6.0. DOS 6.0. Computer Information Systems. Sam's Wholesale Club. Spanish Fluency. Traveled Mexico.

CAREER OBJECTIVE

Corporate finance; with special interest in financial analysis and planning, cash management, capital budgeting and forecasting.

EDUCATION

MASTER OF BUSINESS ADMINISTRATION, June 1994
New York University, New York, NY

Concentration: Finance; Rank: Top 25%.
Vice President: Finance Club; Member: MBA Association

BACHELOR OF SCIENCE IN BUSINESS ADMINISTRATION, May 1992
Elmira College, Elmira, NY

Rank: Top 10% Sigma Iota Epsilon Business Fraternity; substantial concentration in computer information systems.

EXPERIENCE

SUMMER INTERNSHIP, Sam's Wholesale Club, Ft. Lee, NJ, 1993

Under the direction of the Vice-President of Finance.

-- Financial analysis of a cash disbursement system that will increase annual cash flow by $100K.

-- Coordinated and integrated the year-end audit schedules.

-- Assisted in bank relations, float analysis, armored carrier relations.

-- Aided accounting and EDP managers in the development of a computerized system to automate 75% of all manual invoice matching, saving thousand of labor hours annually.

FOUNDER, Squeaky and Clean Cleaning Company, New York, NY September 1993 - September 1994

Worked 25+ hours per week while attending school full-time. Business paid for school expense, gave me experience in selling, advertising, and customer relations.

COMPUTER PROGRAMMER, Department of the Army, Elmira, NY, August 1991 to January 1992.

Worked full-time to pay for college. Selected from national pool to train as civilian computer specialist for Government. On my own, wrote, tested and documented programs on a Burroughs mainframe computer. Volunteered to work as a United Way Fundraiser.

COMPUTER SKILLS

LOTUS 1-2-3, including Macros, DBASE Database software, SPSS statistical package, EXCEL spreadsheet program, COBOL, BASIC. WordPerfect 6.0. DOS 6.0.

SPECIAL INTERESTS

Fluent in Spanish. Traveled extensively in Mexico. Enjoys reading, investments, politics, public speaking, sailing, tennis.

Kay Lynn Adams

1234 Salamander Court   Home: 609 768-1212
Orange, NJ 97394   Message: 609 768-4444

Keywords: Nursing. Health Care. RN. BSN. Princeton. Manager. Middle Management. Geriatric Extended Care. Supervision. Director. Middle Management. Geriatric. Preventative Care. Nursing Home Care Unit. Infection Control. Psycho-Social Care. Teaching. Team Leader.

Seek middle management job in geriatric extended-care facility.

HIGHLIGHTS

Supervision

Coordinated and supervised nursing team responsible for 24-hour care of geriatric patients at extended care home. State rating upped from AA to AAA.

Expanded program of preventive care, hospitalization rate reduced by 20%.

Upgraded anecdotal reporting on nursing care, assuring that reports are adequate for judging staff advancement potential.

Teaching

Taught in-service programs for floor staff on geriatric care issues such as diabetes, psycho-social care needs, infection control, physiology of aging.

Taught "Principals of Home Care" at community college continuing education program.

Planning & Problem Solving

Co-chaired joint committee on infection control and product evaluation involving nurses throughout hospital. Infection rate fell by 45%.

Responsible for assessing staff adherence to policy standards. Disciplinary report rate fell by 30%.

Effectively represented the unique interests and priorities of the nursing home staff. Turnover reduced by 25%.

Continued

EMPLOYMENT HISTORY

1986 to Present	Nursing Manager, Sacred Heart Nursing Home, Orange.
1980 to 1986	Teaching Assistant, School of Nursing, Princeton.
1978 to 1980	Staff Registered Nurse, Grover Medical Center, Newark.

EDUCATION

1978	Bachelor of Science, Nursing, Princeton University.

CONTINUING EDUCATION SAMPLING

1994	Seminar: "New Studies in Aging"
1993	Workshop, two weeks: "New Information on Care of Diabetes."
1992	Evening Course: "Physiology of Older Americans Reevaluated"
1992	In-Service: "Care and Feeding of the Geriatric Patient"

PROFESSIONAL MEMBERSHIPS

1980 - Present	American Nursing Association
1986 - Present	Extended Care Nursing Network, Orange Chapter

BOOKS

1989	"So You Want to Be a Geriatric Nurse," published by Career Visions, Key West, Florida

JOLENE H. GIBBONS
12241 North First Street
Columbus, OH 98000
614 455-5577

KEYWORDS

Human Services. Non-Profit. Program Director. Program Coordinator. Program Advisor. Communications. Coordinator. Project Director. Superintendent. MS Degree. Howard University. BA Psychology. College of William and Mary. Urban League. Strong Interpersonal Skills.

OBJECTIVE

Position as Program Executive in a human services setting.

QUALIFICATIONS

Demonstrated abilities in directing and supervising staff, achieving balance between task needs and volunteers' needs. Supervisor describes me as "Having the uncommon ability to inspire high-performance work and yet maintain a serene environment ... not an easy task with the diverse personalities in our operation."

Rated in performance reviews as "highly effective in analyzing work flow and communications patterns" to maximize effectiveness of the work team.

Skilled and confident in organizing start-up phase of new projects.

College degree in human relations, with 12 years of professional experience.

SAMPLE OF EXPERIENCE

Direct staff of up to 30 people, including counseling, support, security, and clerical personnel in several work environments, such as school, counseling center, community treatment centers, and business.

Train, supervise and **evaluate** staff, enabling them to improve skills and achieve work objectives.

Designed a highly successful and innovative parent-child relations program.

WORK HISTORY

1985 to Present	Coordinator of Volunteers, Audubon National Park Association, Columbus, OH
1976 to 1984	Superintendent, Community Treatment Centers, Cleveland, OH
1974 to 1975	Consultant, Cuyahoga County Resource Center, Cleveland, OH
1972 to 1974	Project Director, Urban League, Billings, MT

EDUCATION

1982	Master of Science, Human Relations Howard University Washington, DC
1980	Bachelor of Arts, Psychology College of William and Mary Williamsburg, VA

PERSONAL PHILOSOPHY

This I believe: Tapping the grass roots through volunteerism and nonprofit endeavors enriches every citizen of America in some way. Although private social service providers are feeling the chill wind of recession, and although the pay is modest and the hours are long, working in human services is meaningful work. What you do matters. Working in human services makes me glad to get up in the morning. If you have an opening for my kind of person, can we talk?

CYNTHIA ANNE McDONALD
2020 West Breeze Way
New London, Connecticut 68434
402 648-5578

Key Words Dietitian. Nutritional Consultant. Director of Nutritional Services. Corporate Food Service Manager. Dietitian. Dietitian Administrator. Teacher. Director. MS Degree. Education. BS Degree. Nutritional Science. Connecticut College.

Objective Corporate Food Service Management.

Offering Creative flair for generating and presenting program ideas.

Ability to inspire others to work at their highest level.

Ability to prioritize and delegate.

Exceptional communications and interpersonal skills, according to three employers.

Twelve years of successful management experience.

Highlights

Management & Supervision

Planned $500,000 food budget and monitored expenses for Child Care food program, maintaining mandatory government records and filing for reimbursement.

Orchestrated complex transportation of 2,300 meals per day to 32 sites from one central kitchen in San Diego.

Supervised staffs of up to 100 employees. Conducted interviewing, hiring, scheduling, attendance control and worker evaluations.

Administration

Coordinated all aspects of the nutritional component of Head Start program for 2,300 children throughout New London County.

Training

Initiated a five-week nutrition education program for recovering patients in an alcohol and substance abuse treatment facility.

Trained teachers in effective teaching techniques with preschool children, and monitored their use of the nutrition curriculum.

Employment History

1986 - Now   Nutrition Consultant, New London Head
                 Start

1982 - 1986   Director of Nutritional Services, New
                 London Hospital

1979 - 1982   Dietitian Administrator, Assembly School
                 District

Education

1980   Master of Science, Education
           Connecticut College, New London, CT

1978   Bachelor of Science, Nutritional Science
           New London State College, New London, CT

COMMENTS ON SELECTED SAMPLE RESUMES

Sean Michael Glenn (Pages 160–162)
Under the old rules, three pages may seem too many for a facilities manager, but Glenn is in a tough job market and is trying to transfer from the public sector into the private sector. He needs to show his superior qualifications in-depth. Computers want all the facts to consider an applicant for more than one job title.

Joshua Jacob Murphy (Pages 165–166)
Although two-column resumes are a mistake, scanning systems can handle brief pairs of items such as Murphy's specific responsibilities.

Lee Ann Jameson (Pages 167–168)
Note how her name appears above the contact information

Stephen J. Sterling (Pages 189–190)
His name is set in 24-point type, much larger than the recommended 10 point to 14 point. Names are an exception to the rule and can be up to 32 point. Otherwise, it's best to stick to the rule.

Gerald E. Raines (Pages 199–200)
The name and contact information are placed in the upper right-hand corner because, when thumbing through stacks of paper, resumes readers tend to look in that spot. These days, you never know *what* or *who* is reading your resume.

Jolene H. Gibbons (Pages 203–204)
The personal philosophy section, strictly for the human gallery, is meant to bolster a fact-short resume.

Marion C. Evans (Pages 178–179)
Notice how Evans includes all her professional affiliations, even though she doesn't indicate a leadership role in any one of them. Nevertheless, the keywords in each organization may result in a computer pulling her name to a computer screen. Do you think she should have included the professional affiliations in her keyword summary?

Jamie Lee Alexander (Page 182)
This keyword summary has extra white space between each keyword. Although not absolutely necessary, the additional white space may be an additional guard against a computer misreading the words. It can't hurt.

CHECKLIST FOR SCANNABLE RESUMES

1. Did I carefully choose the most likely keywords for my resume and arrange them in an appropriate order?

2. Did I use a popular, common typeface?

3. Did I (except for my name) use a font size between 10 points and 14 points?

4. Did I avoid italics, script, and underlined passages?

5. Did I avoid using graphics and shading?

6. Did I use horizontal and vertical lines sparingly and allow a quarter-inch of white space around them?

7. Did I use a 24-pin letter quality or laser printer?

8. Did I use understandable abbreviations? Synonyms?

9. Did I use $8^1/_2$" × 11" white paper?

10. Did I put my name at the very top?

11. Did I avoid stapling or folding my resume?

12. Did I have my resume photocopied in a first-class copier?

13. Am I sending the original copy of my resume?

14. If faxing, did I put the setting on "fine mode"?

The answer to all these questions should be YES!

8

The Video Resume Interview

The Electronic Superhighway Means Resumes in Living Color

"Someday" is almost here for the electronic superhighway with its lanes for television, video telephones, and computers. This chapter looks at a new style of resume—one that talks. It offers tips and scripts for making a top-of-the-line screen debut.

It's coming soon to a screen near you: the video resume. Are you ready?

Video resumes actually were introduced in the early 1960s. Until now, they never caught on because they were too hard to view and too hard to handle. Even recruiters who have a VCR in their offices rarely want to interrupt a busy day to get up, cross the room, load in a tape, and watch an audition. It's not convenient; it's still "taking time out."

That may change. CD-ROM players hooked up to office computers can make video resumes easily accessible in the fairly immediate future.

The idea is simple and is on drawing boards now: After using an automated tracking system to make a preliminary list of candidates, a recruiter can get a better feel for each individual by calling up a video capsule of the candidate, imbedded on a CD-ROM disk.

With an audition, on a disk, just a keystroke away on the recruiter's own desktop computer, watching a video resume becomes a convenience, not one more chore in a heavy-duty day. Hundreds of job seekers can fit on one CD-ROM. It's a snap.

Despite it's amazing capabilities, CD-ROM is regarded as "bridge" technology. In the future, imaging is expected to arrive on an electronic highway that government and industry may work together to build. What some are now calling a "national information infrastructure" will serve as an electronic highway system for home and office computers, telephones, and television.

The video resume should be viewed against the backdrop of this changing technology. You may not need it this very instant, but you may need it quickly in a nearby tomorrow.

Going from the one-dimensional (print or electronics) resume to the video resume will mean reinventing the art of self-marketing. It doesn't take too much imagination to visualize video resume kiosks everywhere (much like today's familiar photo-developing and key-making booths) and an explosion of image consultants to help every candidate come across as a hot prospect.

When you're ready to face the cameras, the best plan is to try your first recording in a commercial videotaping studio.

If you prefer to try a self-produced version, enlist the help of two friends: one to work the camcorder and the other to feed you questions. Choose a setting appropriate to the kind of job you want—an office for white-collar and managerial work, a health lab for lab technologists, the outdoors for foresters, an airport for pilots, and so forth.

Because a video resume is more like an interview than a resume, job interview strategies apply. Let's look at a few examples.

TELL ME ABOUT YOURSELF

Stripped of its mystique, a video interview is really a version of the famous hot-seat request made by interviewers from the day fire was discovered and the discoverer was hoping to get a job as a cook: "Tell me about yourself."

You will have no more than two to five minutes to:

1. Announce your name.
2. Summarize your background.
3. Sell your job skills.
4. Sign off with a thank-you.

You have to do all this without sounding rushed and breathless! To pick up the action and avoid a long, boring, "talking head" video, here is a "script" of how you ("Mike Madison" in this scenario) and your off-camera interviewer might interact.

You: Hello. My name is Mike Madison. I've been in operations research for six years and I'm ready for greater responsibilities.

Interviewer: What about your experience, Mike?

You: For the past three years, I've been at Wonder Corporation, where I've—[the description of measurable achievements should make up the bulk of your video resume].

Interviewer: Were you educated in the Midwest?

You: Yes; I'm a graduate of Iowa University where I majored in management science. It was as an undergraduate that I first became interested in operations research and have made that my career focus. And I'm glad I did because it's a good fit.

Interviewer: Thanks, Mike. How can employers reach you?

[*Slide with Mike's contact information comes onto the screen. Mike reads the contact information aloud while the slide is on the screen.*]

You: Thanks for viewing my resume. Let's talk soon.

ADVANTAGES AND DISADVANTAGES OF VIDEOS

Take a minute to anticipate what a video resume can and can't do for you.

Advantages

1. Because it can do much of the work of the initial screening interview, you aren't as likely to arrange waste-of-time meetings.
2. You can convey your commitment to your career through eye-to-camera contact, body language, and voice tone.
3. It can reverse stereotypes that may be hurting you. For example, a technical person who desires a management position may be perceived as lacking people skills. A positive, vital personality on screen can suggest management potential by showing an interest in people as well as in things.
4. Shipping your video to other cities facilitates long-distance job searches.

5. As long as it's still a novelty, you'll be remembered as "the applicant who used the video resume."

Disadvantages

1. The risk of using a video resume is like the chance you take when you enclose a photo with a paper resume: animated or not, you may jog a negative memory—a dislike that may not arise in person.

2. Jeff Allen (*Jeff Allen's Best: The Resume*) is right when he points out: "Legally, video resumes encourage *un*equal opportunity employers. . . . Race, height, weight, and age should not (and legally *cannot*) be considered in hiring someone . . . you'll encounter discrimination. You just won't know it."

COMMON SENSE SUGGESTIONS

Another career authority, leading New York executive search consultant and author John Lucht (*Rites of Passage at $100,000+*), says you should always remember that you're proving yourself on two levels:

1. A fine person.
2. Someone obviously able to do the job.

Let this dual requirement serve as your litmus test as you prepare your video resume:

1. Am I coming across as a fine person?
2. Am I coming across as someone obviously able to do the job?

Start with appearance. The image that registers in the recruiter's mind as your video is viewed will be one of the most long-lasting determinants of who gets invited in for a face-to-face interview.

Costume yourself for the type of job you seek: a conservative suit for business, a lab coat for lab technology, and so on. Once your grooming and dress are in hand, try to project high energy, alertness, and enthusiasm.

When you need help with your video image, don't decide you can't afford to get assistance. You can't afford *not* to get a coach. You must look and do your best because you won't get a second chance.

To identify professional help, look in the yellow pages telephone directory under "Image Consultants" or "Video Production Services."

ADDITIONAL TIPS

1. Be brief, natural, and specific about your qualifications and achievements.

2. Give facts, figures, and specific job titles. Don't generalize, be too slick, do fancy editing, or make stilted comments.

3. Always wrap a written resume around the clearly labeled videotape or videodisk. If you are sending your video resume individually (rather than having it packaged with others by a third party), never ship the video before calling the employer and explaining what you are sending. Find out whether you should include a return mailing envelope or whether the employer will be responsible for sending it back.

4. Follow up with another call after allowing a reasonable time to view your forceful, compact presentation of your marketing message. Ask for a live interview.

5. If you're turned down, ask for an evaluation of the video resume. Try to find out what the problem is and repair it. Seek referrals: "Do you know of another employer who might be interested in someone with my qualifications? Would it be okay if I use your name?"

SAMPLE VIDEO RESUME SCRIPT

Now that you have a firm grasp of the concept, here's a free-form script of a video resume, to illustrate an approach you might use.

Busby: Hello, my name is Elaine Busby. I'm looking for a scientific or technical writing position with a corporation or university.

Interviewer: Where do you hail from, Elaine?

Busby: I grew up in St. Louis, Missouri. I have a master's degree in economic history from Duke University in North Carolina. My baccalaureate, also in history, is from Rutgers University in New Jersey.

Interviewer: What do you offer an employer, Elaine?

Busby: My bosses say I am highly effective in communication with engineers and technicians. I can translate scientific information into everyday language.

My aim is to focus on scientific and technical communication in a corporate or academic setting.

In my most recent assignment, I prepared 14 technical manuals for worldwide distribution. It took me nine months, which is about half the time expected for this kind of job. I work fast.

In addition to working well with technical personnel and translating scientific information into everyday language, I have analyzed corporate telecommunications needs and written 23 customized proposals.

Interviewer: Have you managed or developed major telecommunications accounts?

Busby: Absolutely! I'm proud of my track record in managing and developing name accounts such as White Lions and Red Rovers.

Interviewer: What about your writing skills?

Busby: I am a published writer in eight trade and professional publications. I've done one book for Abello Publishing titled *Clinical Management of Memory Failure.* And, I have seven years' experience in teaching at a community college.

Interviewer: It sounds like you're a proven technical writer.

Busby: You bet! I am widely experienced at producing reports and business plans for management. I have done hundreds of proposals for clients.

[*Camera pans display of publications*]

In addition, I have written a number of user guides and feature summary sheets for electronic equipment.

[*Camera pans samples*]

I have authored numerous articles and reviewed the works of others. Possibly the most challenging task I've ever tackled was editing a textbook series for high school science students.

[*Elaine points to textbook series, picks up one for camera to see*]

In summary, I offer abilities in technical analysis and presentation, as well as project management and distribution sales. My employment history includes service with such companies as Kerex Corporation, Ultra Dynamics Communications Company, Beam Corporation, and Bruner Communications. The details are in my text resume.

Interviewer: And what is it you want to do, Elaine?

Busby: I'm ready to merge my foundation in technology with my strong writing skills. Can we get together and see how I might bring needed skills to your operation? I appreciate your time from your busy schedule. Thanks. I hope to hear from you soon.

ONE MORE VIDEO RESUME CONCERN

If you are not currently employed, you need not worry about confidentiality. If you are employed, a disguise and an alias, or even the television special effects that mask faces with electronic blocking squares are all available.

All kidding aside, we have no idea how you can prevent word from getting back to your boss that you're ready to jump ship, if you're starring locally in CD-ROM job market productions. A video resume may be safest if you're planning a long-distance move and the tape will be seen by companies in faraway cities.

9

When Computers Don't Give You a Passing Glance

The Answer: Take It Personally

The dazzling technology changing the face of job finding has a dark side. People with low-demand or obsolete skills risk being left by the side of the road as computers help fast-trackers race by on their way to jobs. This concluding chapter offers guidance to those who are passed over by recruiting computers.

Alex Ladue (not his real name), 61, of San Francisco is still looking for employment 17 months after being laid off as director of international sales for a West Coast computer manufacturer. His distinguished career was spent at several famous-name companies. He can handle four foreign languages—French, Portuguese, Spanish, and Italian—and is a Korean War hero. A frequent long-distance cycler, he's physically fit and likely to be assumed to be younger than he is. After living the career dream for a white male in the American Century, Ladue is at loggerheads about what to do next.

His enemy, of course, is age discrimination. "The way it's done is that the application is simply ignored," Ladue says. "When another application is hand-carried, it too just somehow disappears 'in the pile.' One is told there are so many applications and resumes that some simply get lost. Sending applications is getting to feel like a mere waste of postage."

Ladue has another gripe expressed by over-50 workers again and again.

"Perhaps where I feel the most left out is that business seems to have universally turned first contact with applicants over to the inexperienced young, who in not having walked much of life's experiences too often seem quite happy to send you packing and are too ready to remind you they have plenty of other applications and haven't much time for people who are too old and overpaid," he says.

The displaced international sales executive has tried without success to pass through many doors to employment, including those to executive suites. "In the current job climate, the old how-to nostrums about contacting only those at the top just don't work anymore," Ladue believes.

Ladue's age discrimination problems may or may not be solved by the new resume processing and applicant tracking software sweeping America. Omitting information more than ten years in the past will help him make the first several cuts in the screening process. It's a little harder to explain how one's resume or application "got lost in a pile" when it's in a computer database, but clerks so instructed can delete any resume with a couple of keystrokes. (It will be instructive to watch this issue develop over the next several years.)

YOUNG PEOPLE CAN BE SNUBBED BY COMPUTERS TOO

Terry Sanchez (not her real name), 31, lives in Amarillo, Texas, where she struggles with almost unbearable anxiety about what the future holds.

"I'm trying to decide where my career went wrong," Sanchez says. "I have an accounting degree from Texas A&M, one of the largest and most prestigious business schools in my part of the country. However, I have been able to find employment in my field in only three out of the nine-and-a-half years I have been out of school. I have currently been unemployed for about two years. How can I make sense out of my situation?" the unemployed accountant asks.

Unless devilishly well-constructed, a keyword resume isn't going to be a guardian angel for Terry Sanchez. Even if it survives the screening process and gains human evaluation, the stretches of unemployment are likely to knock her out of consideration in a market chock-full of job hunting accountants.

In Duncan, Oklahoma, Sarah Provo (not her real name) says her husband, Kurt, is a biologist who has been working for 11 years as a lab technician in the oil and gas well-drilling industry. Now Kurt wants a "more professional job in the environmental-biological field" but after "sending out resumes for ads in newspapers for two-and-a-half years" he has had no luck.

"We have already sold our home, and are willing to move, including going overseas. It seems like we've gotten nowhere. Two employers interviewed him but more or less told him his skills are obsolete for their environmental biology jobs," Sarah Provo explains, with discouragement lining her face.

The obstacles Kurt faces in upgrading and changing career fields will not be erased by the new technology. As our practical-minded grandparents used to say, "Fix the roof before you paint the house."

Jimmy A. McDaniel (his real name), a career counselor in the criminal justice system, reports he often is asked, "How do I tell them I'm an ex-felon?" The answer for McDaniel's clients is outside the scope of keyword resumes.

Jonas Maxwell (not his real name), 24, says he has an "associate of applied science degree in video production" from a private technical school. No job.

"I have had a hard time finding work in a television station or production company. What," asks Maxwell, "are the best opportunities for a person with this degree?"

Jonas Maxwell's chances of finding work through keyword technology are minimal.

Nadine Mendoza (not her real name), 50, would like to re-enter the world of paid work after an 18-year absence. "I have never felt so unwanted in my life as I have after looking for a job for the past three months. It makes you want to jump off a bridge."

Alex Ladue, Terry Sanchez, Kurt Provo, Jimmy A. McDaniel's clients, Jonas Maxwell, and Nadine Mendoza—all are job seekers who will not be happy travelers on the scannable resume circuits.

Their situations of age discrimination, jagged employment history, obsolete job skills, difficult-to-interpret background, low-demand job skills, and absence of job skills is causing the rejections they face.

For individuals outside the mainstream of today's employment channels, apart from entrepreneurship, five main options are open:

1. Apply to smaller companies that do not yet use automated applicant tracking systems, and hope they are not subscribing to a

commercial service bureau. Companies are automating rapidly, and it is impossible to predict whether small companies will continue to offer millions of employment opportunities. Your guess is as good as ours.

2. Take a temporary job and try to turn it into a permanent position.

3. Look for several part-time permanent jobs. Personnel firms in several cities offer this kind of opportunity, which is especially attractive to high-performing pros who have years of experience.

4. When the wolf is not at the door, you may be able to make a career change into a nonprofit organization by volunteering and hoping to nab a permanent paid spot when one opens.

5. Use personal networking, the answer for most people who can't get past screening computers or humans.

The last option deserves some space of its own.

NETWORKING

Find a personal, human way to get "inside" the interviewing barriers by doing some networking. This contacting technique is dissected in numerous networking guides. Read one or two of them cover-to-cover.

Even in fortress industries—movies, breweries, investment banking, sports—where entrance is based largely on friends hearing about and receiving jobs through friends, there are ways to cross the invisible moats that keep outsiders at a distance.

Most people don't understand how to network effectively. Discuss it at random and people will tell you that networking is a matter of calling up friends, or names sent along by friends, to see whether they have heard of any jobs, or it requires going to meetings to pass around business cards. Networking is much more.

Real networking is carefully tended give-and-take. It's the favor bank into which you make regular deposits as well as take withdrawals. The best networkers practice the preventive networking art over years of concern and caring for their contacts.

When you have a zero balance in the favor bank and need an emergency withdrawal, you'll have to use the shortcuts suggested in the networking guides. What you learn about the scope and variations of using people in your job search may surprise you.

Networking can be as sophisticated as hopping a plane to Honolulu to attend a glamorous national meeting of professionals who can hire you or who can give you hot job leads.

Networking can be as elementary as riding a bicycle from copy shop to copy shop, chatting with the counter attendants, until you find a job.

The common denominator in all networking is human intervention. At the end of the process, you are persuading a third person to access an employer on your behalf.

There is no better way to pass through the interviewing portals than on the coattails of a sponsor. You need a third party who knows the hiring authority well enough to get past the palace guard and deliver the message before the throne: "There's someone you should meet. . . ."

When the machines seem to be beating you, use people to beat the machines.

BECOME EXPERT AT TRACKING JOBS

When you suspect that you've been wronged by the screening technology and that you don't stand a snowball's chance in the hot new world of scannable resumes, finding a good new job is the best revenge.

With the following step-by-step approach, your longed-for fresh start can be within reach.

Money

Consolidate your financial niches. Collect unemployment insurance; see about possible eligibility for COBRA, which permits you to continue your health insurance coverage for 18 months; get exact costs of staying in the company's health plan (or enrolling in another plan) at your own expense; prepare realistic budgets ("lean meat" and "bare bones") and see how your predictable income can be stretched. Many job-search expenses are tax-deductible, so tape your receipts into a notebook and indicate what the money bought.

Confirm Career Direction

Are you sure you wish to continue in the same field, or is a career change indicated? The *Occupational Outlook Handbook*, published by the U.S. Department of Labor, is industrial-strength help. Most libraries have it. It covers about 87 percent of the nation's occupations, giving information on the nature of the work, working conditions, outlook, earnings, related occupations, and information sources.

Tools

Get the necessary technical tools: a telephone answering machine with a remote access capability; a telephone credit card to use when you're away from home; a PC with a word processing program that has a spelling check feature. If you can afford it, a car telephone is helpful for arranging immediate interviews.

Assessment

Inventory and list all your accomplishments as they relate to what you want to do. Next to each accomplishment, identify the skills you used. You'll be matching your skills with a potential employer's need or problem, so spend time on this. It's the basis of your self-marketing. If your skills are obsolete or not up to market strength, you'll have to lower your expectations until you can build or renew your skills.

Marketing Materials

Prepare your paper nonscannable resume. Have simple personal cards printed with your name and contact information to give to those you meet in networking forays. Tip: Instead of printing that you're an accountant or retail manager, personalize your cards by handwriting your occupation as you give them out. It's a matter of style.

Gather Job Leads

Review your Rolodex, Christmas card list, associations, friends of friends—call to mind everyone you know. Read job hunt books on how to use your contacts to target possible jobs. Collect recruitment ads from newspapers and trade publications; learn to analyze in detail what the advertiser seeks and ask yourself whether you've got it.

If you can ferret out the name of the person who will make a hiring decision, try to network your way to an appointment with that person rather than sending a resume and letter. If you can obtain a job description, you're way ahead of the competition. Compile a list of target employers, and use new research techniques to gather detailed data on each company. (Our companion book, *Electronic Job Search Revolution*, devotes a chapter to using the new electronic employer databases to compile lists of blue-ribbon job prospects and learn what those prospects are up to in this changing world.)

Dialing for Dollars

Telemarketing yourself—canvasing for job interviews—is one of the most efficient ways of looking for work, but it's not something everyone can do or should do. In this situation, you should call hiring decision makers, not human resource specialists. You'll need to get the names from company switchboards.

You may be stonewalled if you ask in a direct manner for the name of the target manager. Instead of asking, "Who is the manager of quality control?," ask, "Is John Raymond the manager of quality control?" You'll usually be given the correct name ("No, that's Tina Smith.") or the correct title ("No, Mr. Raymond is vice president of marketing."). Ask to be put through or call back later to the person you're targeting for your resume.

What we just described is "cold calling." "Warm calling," a product of networking, allows you to use a third-party referral, "Alex Lithium suggested I call you."

In cold calling, you are contacting strangers. Warm calling is much easier because you've crossed the moat on a bridge marked "mutual friend."

Cold calling may be necessary when you are in real trouble, and referrals developed in cold calling may lead to warm calling.

Cold calling is inappropriate for upper-level professionals and executives.

"Hello, my name is Lee Iacocca and I'm looking for a job as a corporate CEO" would draw guffaws and be labeled a practical joke.

Cold calling is also wrong for those who lack adequate verbal skills or whose self-esteem is easily punctured. Applying to one employer after another can hammer your ego to a pulp because you frequently are treated like an annoying intruder who meets untold rejections in what one researcher calls a "time-consuming, frustrating, and even soul-destroying experience."

You can cold call from lists of prospective employers you line up in the telephone yellow pages, in commercial job-bank books that list employers in a given city, and in employer lists found in print or electronic library business directories.

Plan your script. Like an actor, practice speaking it aloud. After identifying yourself, mention the type of work you're seeking, "I'm interested in discussing how some ideas I've worked out might contribute to economy in your office administration." Try to avoid saying the word "job" in your first sentence so that you are not cut off like a timeshare condo seller.

Quickly follow up with headline sales points, "I have strong work credentials and have received several promotions. My references are outstanding." Next, throw in a "hook" statement, "I initiated a new computer set-up that saved the company many thousands of dollars."

Get ready to close with an affirmation of your personal qualities, "I get along with people and am hard-working and flexible." Close with a request for what you want—an interview, "I really believe it would be mutually beneficial if we could meet and talk. When would be the best time?"

If you are telemarketing from a roster of an association to which you belong, your message can be even briefer. "In my search for employment as an office administrator, whom should I be talking to?" You want several names from each contact, more names from those contacts, and so on.

If telemarketing is a disagreeable thought, two actions can help: (1) find a telemarketing buddy and exchange pep talks once or twice a day; (2) study the scripting in job search books for accessing decision makers, overcoming objections, and salvaging turndowns until you depersonalize the chore and consider it just another way of generating job offers.

Learn to Close

Everything you do until you land an actual job interview is a warmup. The interview is the game, set, and match. You win or you lose. Read up on interviewing and practice with a camcorder until you are a good interviewee. Salespeople have a saying: "He doesn't know how to close." That means the person doesn't know how to ask for the order and comes away without it. In your case, the "order" is a job offer.

Interviewing is an art you don't learn overnight, and nothing, absolutely nothing, replaces practice. Go over and over your practice videotapes. Search for places in your performance that need improvement.

THE CRYSTAL–BARKLEY METHOD OF JOB FINDING

Another philosophy of job tracking deserves a special mention: the Crystal–Barkley method. It was developed by the late John Crystal, an original thinker, in concert with his business partner, Nella Barkley.

Crystal–Barkley is the source of the famous "proposal" method of job hunting, in which your services are valued much like a product in any other business package.

In the Crystal–Barkley approach, you aim your efforts solely at *creating* the job you want, rather than reacting to what others say they want. John Crystal often advised clients, "Get up off your knees and negotiate."

After thinking through what you want to do, the next step is to gather information from which you design a hiring proposal, a request that a company take you on to achieve a defined and needed function. You approach employers with your hiring proposal—the equivalent of a business proposal, often stating a financial or production-increase goal and a general time-frame for its accomplishment.

You are suggesting that an employer—whose needs you can fill—create, or amend, a position built around your proposal. The strategy works, but *it must be expertly implemented*. Read the details in Nella Barkley's top-deck book of guidance, *How To Help Your Child Land the Right Job (Without Being a Pain in the Neck)*. Any job seeker can benefit from this first book written for parents of grown children who are floundering and who perhaps have come back home to live.

If you decide to pursue a proposal style of job search, we can't think how a computer scannable resume will be useful. Getting someone to create a job for you is a person-to-person challenge. You'll need strong presentation and persuasion skills, and confidence that you can meet the proposal's goals.

GOOD FORTUNE CAN BE YOURS

With organization, perseverance, and commitment to excellence, your search won't lose out to the technology that's forever changing the way jobs find people and people find jobs.

Some good opportunities will always be captured the old-fashioned way. When you sense that you are missing out because technology is not your friend, believe in your worth as a *person*. Unlike dinosaurs, the wonders that are people will always tread the earth.

Index

AAP-2672

650.14Ke383e

Kennedy, Joyce Lain.

Electronic resume
revolution : create a
c1994.

DATE DUE
